TESTING
AND
COGNITION

TESTING AND COGNITION

Edited by

Merlin C. Wittrock • Eva L. Baker

Graduate School of Education
University of California, Los Angeles

PRENTICE HALL
Englewood Cliffs, New Jersey 07632

Library of Congress Cataloging-in-Publication Data

Testing and cognition / edited by Merlin C. Wittrock and Eva L. Baker.
    p. cm.
    Includes bibliographical references and index.
    ISBN 0-13-906991-7
    1. Cognition. 2. Educational tests and measurements.
    I. Wittrock, M. C. (Merlin C.), 1931- . II. Baker, Eva L.
    BF311.T39 1991
    371.2′6 — dc20   90-47606
                                                                        CIP

Editorial/production supervision and
  interior design: Fred Dahl
Manufacturing buyers: Debbie Kesar, Mary Ann Gloriande

Copyright © 1991 by the Regents of the University of California
Published by Prentice-Hall, Inc., A Division of Simon & Schuster
Englewood Cliffs, New Jersey 07632

Printed in the United States of America
10 9 8 7 6 5 4 3 2 1

ISBN 0-13-906991-7

Prentice-Hall International (UK) Limited, *London*
Prentice-Hall of Australia Pty. Limited, *Sydney*
Prentice-Hall Canada Inc., *Toronto*
Prentice-Hall Hispanoamericana, S.A., *Mexico*
Prentice-Hall of India Private Limited, *New Delhi*
Prentice-Hall of Japan, Inc., *Tokyo*
Simon & Schuster Asia Pte. Ltd., *Singapore*
Editora Prentice-Hall do Brasil, Ltda., *Rio de Janeiro*

CONTENTS

LIST OF
CONTRIBUTORS

Eva L. Baker, Graduate School of Education, University of California, Los Angeles, California 90024

Serena Clayton, Graduate School of Education, University of California, Los Angeles, California 90024

Kevin Collis, Faculty of Education, University of Tasmania, Box 252 GPO, Hobert, Tasmania, Australia 7001

Marie Freeman, Graduate School of Education, University of California, Los Angeles, California 90024

Robert Glaser, Learning Research and Development Center, University of Pittsburgh, Pittsburgh, Pennsylvania 15213

Joan L. Herman, Center for the Study of Evaluation, University of California, Los Angeles, California 90024

Barbara L. McCombs, Mid-Continent Regional Laboratory, 12500 E. Iliff Avenue, Aurora, Colorado 80014

Debra K. Meyer, Department of Educational Psychology, University of Texas, Austin, Texas 78712

Thomas A. Romberg, Research and Development Center, University of Wisconsin, 1025 W. Johnson Street, Madison, Wisconsin 53706

Robert J. Sternberg, Department of Psychology, Yale University, New Haven, Connecticut 06520

Claire E. Weinstein, Department of Educational Psychology, University of Texas, Austin, Texas 78712

Merlin C. Wittrock, Graduate School of Education, University of California, Los Angeles, California 90024

PREFACE

This volume explores implications of recent research in cognition for the improvement of educational testing. The first chapter, "Cognition and Testing," by Merlin C. Wittrock, develops some of the differences in perspective toward teaching and testing that follow from cognitive theories and research. He identifies four areas—student preconceptions, processes of learning and comprehension, metacognition, and affective thought processes (motivation and anxiety)—that have contributed to refined concepts of intelligence and knowledge acquisition and use. The import for testing of theory and research in these areas is discussed.

The second chapter, "Testing and Recent Research in Cognition," by Merlin C. Wittrock, reviews recent contributions of cognitive research in attention, motivation, comprehension, learning strategies, and metacognition. After reviewing the research, he discusses some of its implications for educational testing.

The third chapter, "Expertise and Assessment," by Robert Glaser, develops implications for educational assessment from cognitive theory and psychometric theory. He shows how these two areas lead to student assessment procedures that measure students' abilities to learn further material.

For example, the ability to write should be assessed by the students' ability to use writing to articulate arguments, clarify concepts, and to contribute to further learning in school.

The fourth chapter, "Toward Better Intelligence Tests," by Robert J. Sternberg, presents a cognitive model of the mental processes, strategies, and representations that underlie intelligent thinking. After the presentation of the model, he discusses implications for improving testing in education.

The fifth chapter, "Implications of Cognitive Psychology for Testing: Contributions from Work in Learning Strategies," by Claire E. Weinstein and Debra K. Meyer, presents cognitive research on learning strategies and applies it to the improvement of tests in schools. The chapter also discusses research on learning strategies and metacognition that is needed to develop new and better educational tests.

The sixth chapter, "The Definition and Measurement of Primary Motivational Processes," by Barbara L. McCombs, discusses recent theory and empirical research on affective processes, especially motivation and self-efficacy, that have implications for developing tests for use in educational settings. In this chapter, Dr. McCombs presents a model of motivation and self-regulated learning. She discusses its utility in the design of educational tests, in the assessment of cognitive abilities, and in the selection of research needed to develop further applications of cognitive psychology to education.

In the seventh chapter, "Assessment of Mathematical Performance: An Analysis of Open-Ended Test Items," Kevin Collis and Thomas A. Romberg apply theory and research from cognitive psychology to the improvement of assessment procedures in the teaching of mathematics. Tests, such as multiple-choice examinations, measure individual mathematical skills well. However, the measurement of the relationships among concepts in mathematics involves measuring comprehension, learning strategies, and metacognitive processes. Collis and Romberg discuss several practical techniques appropriate for assessing the understanding of mathematics.

In the eighth chapter, "Cognitive Assessment of History for Large-Scale Testing," Eva L. Baker, Marie Freeman, and Serena Clayton discuss recent research conducted on the assessment of comprehension in history and social science. These studies focus on applying cognitive research to the design of tests of understanding information taught in history and in related social science courses. They explore new ways to write and to grade essay questions. These test questions are designed to measure the relationships among concepts and events that comprise comprehension of social science.

In the ninth chapter, "Research in Cognition and Learning: Implications for Achievement Testing Practice," Joan L. Herman synthesizes many of the ideas introduced by the authors of the chapters of this book. She draws practical implications for the revising and improving of assessment procedures in schools. She indicates that assessment procedures in schools will change when they focus upon using testing to improve instruction, rather than to compare students' relative achievement status. These changes in assessment procedures should provide teachers with information that they can use to diagnose learning problems and to design effective teaching strategies.

Merlin C. Wittrock
Eva L. Baker

TESTING
AND
COGNITION

ONE

COGNITION
AND TESTING

Merlin C. Wittrock

This introductory chapter discusses the import for testing
of recently developed models of cognition. In cognitive
models, students' thought processes mediate the effects of
teaching upon achievement. Learning and knowledge acquisition become generative or constructive processes in which
students learn by using their knowledge and their intellectual and affective thought processes to create meaning from
instruction.

Within this context, testing performs useful roles in addition to its customary ones. Testing contributes diagnostic
information about student preconceptions, comprehension
strategies, attributions, and planning or metacognitive processes. Test information in those areas can be used by
teachers to design and to present instruction that will interest learners and that will build upon their knowledge and
thought processes.

COGNITIVE MODELS OF TEACHING

The recent research in cognitive psychology has produced sophisticated and useful ways to conceptualize how teaching influences student achievement (Wittrock, 1986, 1978). According to the cognitive models growing from this recent research, teaching influences achievement through changing the ways students think about, organize, and process information, including how they relate it to their experience and knowledge, and how they apply it to their daily lives. The research indicates that teaching influences achievement by inducing students to construct meaning from the instructions.

These cognitive conceptions of teaching have import for test development and for testing in the following ways. First, student preconceptions — for example, their models of electricity, their models of forces acting on moving objects, and their models of how our economy functions — play critical roles in teaching. According to recent cognitive models of instruction, teaching is the process of leading students to revise and improve their conceptions and beliefs. Teaching goes beyond the presenting or the covering of the subject matter, to include assessing and knowing about students' knowledge and thought processes and devising instruction that will build upon this knowledge.

In these cognitive models, the students' background of knowledge provides the base from which teachers build learning, interest, and understanding. Student preconceptions determine what the learners will be able to understand. Because of the critical role of student preconceptions in instruction, tests need to be designed to supply useful information about them.

Second, the students' processes of learning information — their learning strategies and their methods of knowledge acquisition — play critical roles in mediating the effects of teaching upon achievement in school. Student learning processes include strategies for learning, such as how to read with understanding; how to add and subtract numbers; how to direct attention; how to study; how to remember names, dates, and places; and how to apply knowledge to everyday living. These learning strategies influence how students will try to make sense of information and knowledge presented by their teachers, how learners will relate it to their conceptions, and how they will use it. The sense, or interpretation, they construct from their teachers' presentations influences the students' achievements in school. Teachers need to know their students' learning strategies in order to influence their use. The implications in this area for testing include the development of diagnostic tests that will measure student learning strategies involved in the construction of meaning from information presented in the classroom.

Third, metacognition, the awareness and control of one's thought processes, plays an important role in determining how teaching influences student achievement. Metacognitive processes include the students' ways of monitoring their reading comprehension, of planning their studying, or planning how they will relate information to previously acquired knowledge, of planning how they will apply what they learned, and of planning how they will evaluate their use of learning strategies. Metacognition is an area in which test development can contribute to the improvement of teaching through the enhancement of student self-control of learning.

Fourth, affective thought processes, such as motivation and anxiety, contribute significantly to mediating the effects of teaching upon achievement. The recent research on student attributions for learning, and on the separate processes of worry and emotionality in anxiety, lead to important implications for improving testing. For example, the attributions of learners influence their expectations, interests, and their persistence at studying and at learning. If students attribute their success in school to their effort, they are likely to continue to try to learn, even in the face of failure. If they attribute their success in school to factors over which they have little or no control, such as luck or heredity, they are not likely to persist, even when they have been successful and have been rewarded for their success.

In brief, in cognitive models of instruction, teaching affects student achievement through influencing the learners' cognitive and affective thought processes. Teaching does not usually affect student achievement directly or automatically. What students learn from teachers depends upon the students' background knowledge, learning strategies, metacognitive processes, and affective thought processes.

IMPORT FOR TESTING

One import of cognitive models for testing is that all four types of student thought processes need to be measured and understood because of their central role in the understanding of school achievement. In addition, student thought processes should be measured because teachers can facilitate them through the questions they ask, the directions they give, the contexts they provide, the examples they cite or ask the students to generate, and the strategies they model.

Many standardized intelligence tests, achievement tests, and ability tests were designed for other purposes. They were not designed to measure these diagnostically useful cognitive and affective thought processes. Standardized tests provide valuable information for selecting and placing students and for comparing students, schools, and school districts with one another. These types of data will continue to be useful for their intended purposes of selection, placement, and comparison. However, these tests do not measure student conceptions, learning strategies, or metacognitive or affective thought processes relevant to instruction.

To measure these thought processes of learners as a way to understand better how teaching affects student achievement, I see a need for a complementary type of test information that requires a new type of test. The new type of test would provide diagnostic information about students' preconceptions, learning strategies, and metacognitive and affective thought processes involved in the construction of meaning from instruction. These tests would not provide information useful for comparing achievements of different students, schools, systems, states, or nations. That is not their purpose.

These tests of cognitive processes would provide information relevant to the diagnosis of student learning and to the design and improvement of classroom teaching through an understanding of how students learn. In the following chapters, these implications for improving teaching through the development of tests of cognitive processes are presented and developed further.

REFERENCES

WITTROCK, M.C. (1978). The cognitive movement in instruction. *Educational Psychologist, 13,* 87–95.
WITTROCK, M.C. (1986). Students' thought processes. In M.C. Wittrock (Ed.), *Handbook of research on teaching* (3rd ed.). New York: Macmillan.

TWO

TESTING AND RECENT RESEARCH IN COGNITION

Merlin C. Wittrock

In this chapter, Merlin C. Wittrock discusses some of the educationally relevant recent research in cognition, especially in the areas of attention, attribution, comprehension, and student preconceptions. From the research in these areas, he develops implications for improving educational testing, especially diagnostic testing. He maintains that measures of students' preconceptions, their learning and comprehension strategies, and their attributional and metacognitive processes can contribute diagnostic information useful for the design of instruction and for the improvement of the teaching of subject matter.

INTRODUCTION

Since Alfred Binet and Theophile Simon developed a test for predicting and selecting children who could succeed in conventionally taught classes in schools, many educational tests have focused on measuring the products of learning, the academic achievements of students. These useful tests of intelligence, achievement, and aptitude measure what students know and can do; but only indirectly do they measure how students learn, think, make decisions, and acquire, remember, and apply knowledge gained from instruction.

In contrast, within the last 20 years much psychological and educational research has focused upon understanding, explaining, and enhancing knowledge acquisition and school achievement through identifying and measuring learners' and teachers' cognitive and affective thought processes, such as perception, motivation, attention, comprehension, learning strategies, and metacognition. Studies of these student and teacher thought processes represent a major portion of recent research in cognitive psychology applied to education.

One implication of the recent research on student and teacher cognitive and affective thought processes is that well-constructed measures of student cognitive processes can provide new test information useful to classroom teachers for understanding learners, for diagnosing learning difficulties, and for improving instruction in schools. The recent research on attention, learning strategies, metacognition, attribution, and comprehension, especially in mathematics, science, and reading, indicates strong possibilities of improving teaching through the development of tests of student affective and cognitive processes directly involved in achievement.

In this chapter I develop the implications for testing that stem from the recent research in cognition. I also identify student cognitive processes useful for understanding how students learn subject matter and for developing tests needed to improve teaching. The basic point of the chapter is that the information about student cognitive processes offers possibilities for improving teaching and student achievement through increasing teachers' understanding of students' preconceptions, background knowledge, learning strategies, and metacognitive processes.

RECENT RESEARCH IN COGNITION

Attention

In the recent study of attention, several educationally useful and measurable constructs have been discovered, such as sustained, voluntary attention. Students with learning disabilities, children who are hyperkinetic, and mentally retarded children frequently show deficiencies in voluntary sustained attention, but not in involuntary, short-term attention (Wittrock, 1986b). This finding has important diagnostic and remedial implications which have led to sizable gains on standardized achievement tests. Douglas, Parry, Martin, and Garson (1976) taught seven- and eight-year-old children with attention deficit disorders (i.e., hyperkinetic children) a strategy for controlling their attention. After three months of attention training, the children's scores, compared with those of a comparable group of control children, increased on standardized tests of reading achievement, including oral comprehension and listening comprehension, on the Matching Familiar Figures Test, and on tests of organization and planning.

Malamuth (1979) used cognitive training techniques to increase sustained attention among poor readers who were not hyperactive. Reading scores of the experimental group increased, indicating that the ability to sustain attention may also be a factor in reading achievement among students who are not hyperkinetic or mentally retarded.

In other contexts, attention has been shown (1) to correlate more highly with achievement than does time on task (Peterson & Swing, 1982), and (2) to explain many of the effects of questions and objectives given to students (Wittrock & Lumsdaine, 1978). From these different lines of research there is ample reason to explore the possibilities of using measures of student attention to improve achievement in school through diagnosing students' attentional processes and through using this information to design instruction.

Some measures of voluntary attention exist in the research literature. Unfortunately, many of them involve psychophysiological measures, such as electrocardiographs (EEGs), evoked potentials (EPs), and event-related potentials (ERPs). These measures are more appropriate for laboratory studies of attention than they are for widespread use in education. However, measures of attention that indicate whether students are focusing at the level of meaning or comprehension during reading, and whether they are using a phonological strategy, or a visual or spatial strategy during reading individual words, have been developed and used experimentally (Posner & Friedrich, 1986). Piontkowski and Calfee (1979) offer some classroom techniques for indicating the level of meaning at which the child's attention is focused.

Some tests of attention have been used in research on cognition, such as the Matching Familiar Figures Test, and visual selective attention tests (Avolio, Alexander, and Barrett, 1981). A few tests are available commercially. However, research is needed to develop tests of attention that could be used in school at different grade levels and with different subject matters.

Motivation

In recent research on motivation, comparable advances have been made in knowledge about student attributional processes and their relationships to achievement in schools (Weiner, 1979). Because this important topic is discussed in a separate section of this report, it is only introduced here. Several studies (Dweck, 1975; deCharms, 1972) of attributional change programs have shown large increases in achievement in schools. These increases in achievement tend to occur when the students are taught to believe that, through effort in applying their ability toward learning, they can succeed in school—they will learn. In other words, they, and sometimes their teachers, learn to take a major responsibility for learning in school, to take control over the use of strategies for learning in school (McCombs, 1982).

A number of well-developed and widely used tests of attributions and locus of control are commercially available. Many of these are reprinted in the appendix of a book on motivation (Lefcourt, 1982). The study of motivation, especially attribution and self-efficacy, offers much promise for developing educationally useful diagnostic tests of student thought processes that influence achievement. See Metalsky and Abramson (1981) for a discussion of tests of belief-based and evidence-based attributional styles.

Comprehension

A myriad of studies on reading comprehension gives clear evidence of the increases in reading achievement produced by teaching students to use strategies and metacognitive processes as they read stories or tests. Only a few of these studies will be mentioned here. In the section of this report on learning strategies, additional studies are discussed. See also the *Handbook of Research on Teaching* (Wittrock, 1986b), especially the chapters by Calfee and by Wittrock; Wittrock (1981 and 1986a); recent books on the teaching of reading comprehension, such as McNeil (1987) and Pearson (1985), for further discussion of this voluminous research.

In the studies on the teaching of reading comprehension in schools, students are often taught (1) to relate their knowledge and experience to the text, or (2) to organize the parts of the text or the story into coherent wholes (Wittrock, 1990). For example, Linden and Wittrock (1981) taught elementary school children to use sentences and imagery to generate relations between the texts and their experience. Compared with a comparable group of control children, comprehension increased about 50%, from a posttest mean of 18 for the control group to posttest means of 29 and 31 in the two experimental groups. In a study with about 500 junior high school students, Doctorow, Wittrock, and Marks (1978) doubled reading comprehension in the experimental group, compared with randomly assigned control groups, by having them generate summary sentences, using headings inserted in the text.

Au (1977) taught Hawaiian elementary school children, whose reading scores averaged two standard deviations below the mean, to relate their knowledge and experience to the native Hawaiian stories read to them in class. After one year of instruction in this and related comprehension techniques, the experimental group scored at the 69th percentile on the *Gates-*

MacGinite Reading Test, compared with the three control groups' average percentile ranks of 27, 21, and 8 on the same test. These and other studies provide evidence for the possibilities of increasing reading achievement through the teaching of strategies for directing and controlling comprehension processes.

Student Models and Preconceptions

The models and beliefs that students bring to instruction influence what they will learn and how they can best be taught. Researchers in science education and mathematics learning have studied these student knowledge structures and strategies extensively during the past years. In elementary school science (Osborne & Wittrock, 1983, 1985), children have definite models or preconceptions about how DC current flows in a simple, electrical circuit. Teaching them the scientists' view of the current flow, that is, teaching them the subject matter in the conventional mode of explanation, demonstration, and laboratory experimentation, most often results in poor learning. Students tend to believe that their models are true in the real world—the world outside school—regardless of what they see performed in school by the teachers.

Children in major parts of the English-speaking world appear to have a finite set (three or four) of models about this phenomenon. Similarly, children have only a few different models of concepts such as "animal."

At present, we have developed a few measures, usually obtained in interviews, of these models. Because knowledge about these models changes science teaching, we need to develop and to use simple and inexpensive measures that will diagnose the students' preconceptions.

Although the research on identifying student preconceptions in other areas, such as social science, is relatively recent, it too promises to offer sizable improvements in teaching. These measures of student preconceptions can provide invaluable information to teachers about where to focus their instruction. With this knowledge, teaching becomes something more than covering the subject matter. It becomes a process of leading the learners to generate more useful and accurate models of events in the physical and social sciences.

Considerable progress has occurred recently in measuring student cognitive structures before and after instruction (Shavelson, 1974; Naveh-Benjamin, McKeachie, Lin, & Tucker, 1986) in physics, psychology, and mathematics. Although these techniques measure cognitive structure, not cognitive processes, they represent a valuable contribution to the improvement of instruction through the application of research on cognitive psychology. They also provide useful ideas for the design of testing programs.

In mathematics learning (e.g., Brown & Vanlehn, 1982) the measurement of children's addition and subtraction strategies promises a significant improvement in our ability to diagnose learning difficulties and to design instruction appropriately for the children's specific problems. Measures of strategies children use to solve these problems are needed, not only in addition and subtraction, but in other areas of mathematics, and eventually in other subjects as well. The potential for improving educational testing, and consequently teaching, through the development of these process measures is enormous.

Through research on these cognitive processes, sizable gains have been reported in student achievement in a variety of subject matter areas, including reading, mathematics, and science. [See Wittrock, 1986b, for further discussions of these studies, including student perceptions of instruction, attention, attribution, comprehension, learning strategies, and metacognitive processes.]

The fundamental cognitive model of learning underlying these recent advances, which leads to basic changes in the design and conduct of research on teaching, assumes that the effects of instruction depend upon students' strategies and preconceptions (Osborne & Wittrock, 1983) and upon the students' and the teachers' interpretations and understanding of instruction (Wittrock, 1974, 1978). This model has implications for improving our understanding of basic learning constructs. For example, reinforcers may not work automatically (as has been believed), but may increase learning, motivation, and persistence primarily because students attribute them to their own effort, not to luck, other people, or even to their ability. Research on attribution theory has repeatedly made this point in multiple educational contexts and subject matters. Further, a teacher's praise of a student seems to influence the attention of many students who observe it, rather than serving primarily to reinforce the behavior of the student given the accolade by the instructor. Praise serves to direct the attention of many students through observational learning, not automatically through contingent administrations of it by teachers (Brophy, 1981).

In related ways, student attention better predicts achievement than does time on task. The self-fulfilling prophecy occurs primarily when students perceive and act upon the differential treatment a teacher gives them. That finding explains why only some students in a class show the self-fulfilling prophecy. It is a dyadic process, depending upon students' thoughts and feelings, not a uniform, classwide effect that depends only upon the teacher's actions.

Reading comprehension also has been shown to depend upon the meanings students actively generate as they read (e.g., Wittrock, 1981). The background knowledge, learning strategies, and metacognitive processes of students mediate the comprehension they generate from instruction.

Cognitive psychologists are also investigating ways to evaluate the teaching of learning strategies and metacognition, two topics of interest and importance to teachers because of their potential for enhancing transfer of learning.

Metacognition and Learning Strategies

Learning strategies refer to the cognitive processes people use to enhance their acquisition and retention of information and knowledge, such as constructing summaries and inferences to enhance reading comprehension, or generating interactive images to facilitate memory of factual information (Weinstein & Mayer 1986). Metacognition, or metacognitive processes, refers to the awareness and control of one's thought processes, such as the planned development and use of a sequence of learning strategies to enhance attention, knowledge acquisition, retention, or performance.

Research on metacognition and learning strategies interests educators because of its potential for teaching thinking skills and its potential for facilitating transfer of learning from one course, topic, or subject to another, and from school contests to everyday problems at home and at work. Transfer of learning does not come easily. Teachers' attempts to teach for transfer have often ended in disappointment. Transfer does not seem to be a natural or automatic occurrence, at least with the costly and time-consuming procedures commonly employed by teachers.

Research on metacognition and learning strategies offers a useful approach toward the teaching of transfer and toward the teaching of thinking skills either embedded in subjects and curricula or taught as a separate generalizable process. The research on learning strategies and metacognition implies that transfer occurs when we have taught students to be aware of their thought processes and to plan to use them to organize and to understand information and to relate it to other school subjects and to their everyday lives. These processes are also fundamental to comprehension, which involves constructing relations across concepts and relations between subject matter and practical, out-of-school situations. Comprehension, in this sense, is fundamental to transfer of learning.

The teaching of learning strategies and metacognition promises sizable dividends for improving comprehension and transfer of learning (Keogh & Glover, 1980). The reason is that many students do not use these processes spontaneously. Adult illiteracy usually involves a lack of proficiency in comprehension strategies and in metacognition. Over several years, Wittrock and Kelly (1984) studied several hundred young, functionally illiterate adults. Nearly all of them could decode words, but very few of them used, monitored, or evaluated learning strategies and metacognitive processes. In these experiments, when learning strategies and metacognitive processes were taught to these students, their reading comprehension, including their ability to read on-the-job technical text, improved substantially—about 20%. In other studies of reading comprehension among elementary school and high school students, the teaching of learning strategies and metacognitive processes (e.g., write summaries, relate the text to your experience, construct images, draw inferences) regularly increases reading comprehension by about 50%, sometimes by 100% (e.g., Linden & Wittrock, 1981; Doctorow, Wittrock, & Marks, 1978). Among college students, similar but smaller effects have been found (Wittrock & Alesandrini, in press).

Other researchers report related findings. Capelli and Markman (1982) found that when students read they do not integrate or organize material into units that could facilitate transfer. Neither do they generate hypotheses, inferences, expectations, or interpretations. Bransford, Sherwood, Vye, and Rieser (1986) report that students do not often use information learned as facts to solve problems. The information should be associated in class to the situations and events the students will likely encounter later if one wants it to be used later to solve problems.

Donald Meichenbaum (1981) summarized studies on cognitive-behavioral approaches to educational interventions. He categorically states that students in these studies do not use metacognition. They usually learn without intent to use the information later, without perceiving its relations to other contexts. They do not monitor their learning strategies or deliberately plan effective learning and comprehension strategies.

Metacognitive and Learning-Strategy Training that Facilitates Transfer

I have already described the Wittrock and Kelly (1984), Doctorow, Wittrock & Marks (1978), and Linden and Wittrock (1981) studies with adults and elementary school children that regularly produce 20% to 100% gains in reading comprehension and transfer by teaching students to use metacognition and learning strategies. Other researchers produce closely related findings. Brown, Campione, and Day (1981) found that transfer occurs when students use comprehension strategies. Palinscar and Brown (1984) gave metacognitive training to students and sizably enhanced comprehension of material in the children's textbooks.

Keogh and Hall (1984) reviewed training programs in special education that produce transfer. The programs that produced the best transfer provided strategy training across different tasks. Butterfield and Belmont (1977) and Belmont, Butterfield, and Ferretti (1982) provide support for the importance of training "executive" functions of cognition to produce transfer. These executive functions include the construction of goals and plans and the monitoring of their implementation.

The Testing and Evaluation of Metacognition

Research in cognition has developed procedures for measuring and evaluating the effects of teaching students to use learning strategies and metacognition (Sternberg, 1981). The measurement of these processes involves quantifying student procedural knowledge, including ways of acquiring, transferring, and applying information and strategies learned in schools to subjects ranging from history and geography to mathematics and science.

Some of these procedures involve measuring verbal and imaginal learning and metacognition. Others involve procedures for quantifying the organization and cognitive structure of the knowledge students have acquired, along with the relations between that knowledge and the everyday contexts to which it applies. Some examples of this first type of procedure are (1) think alouds, (2) protocol analyses, and (3) stimulated recall. Examples of the second category are: (1) semantic networks, (2) semantic maps, (3) ordered trees, (4) graphic organizers, (5) concept maps, (6) summaries, and (7) frame structures.

These procedures provide diagnostically useful information about how students learn, how they organize information, how they relate it to other knowledge, including their preconceptions, and how they apply it to everyday contexts. These kinds of information provide data, different from conventional achievement tests, that relate directly to furthering our understanding of how students go about their learning and of how teachers might facilitate those processes to increase comprehension and transfer (Wittrock, 1987)

All these examples of application of cognitive learning models imply that researchers and teachers need to measure the cognitions and affects that students use differentially to generate meaning from experience, to construct knowledge from instruction, and to build sensitivity and feeling from the liberal arts and sciences. The implications for testing of these cognitive models deserve further research and development because of their potential contribution to the improvement of teaching.

IMPLICATIONS FOR TESTING AND TEACHING

The research on cognition discussed in the previous section leads to a number of important implications for assessment. It raises the possibility of measuring processes that mediate learning and achievement, and of using these measures to provide diagnostic information to improve instruction. By assessing how students process information, potential problem areas can be identified and remediated. Because students' background knowledge, comprehension strategies, learning strategies, and metacognitive processes mediate the comprehension that students generate from instruction, measures of these thought processes are useful for designing instruction appropriate for different learners. Research on these measurement problems could enrich our concept of testing in schools, could improve our model of how instruction influences achievement, and could lead to the creation of new types of tests of student thought processes to complement achievement tests. School teachers want and would use these types of test information.

**TABLE 2.1   Percentages of Teachers Who Want Test Information
About Reading Strategies**

READING STRATEGIES	PERCENT OF TEACHERS
Obtaining the main idea	90.7
Drawing inferences	86.0
Ability to analyze	81.4
Generalizing from the text	72.1
Ability to synthesize	69.8
Organizing information in the text	69.8
Reading critically	69.8
Constructing summaries	65.1
Generating questions about the text	58.1
Relating text to prior knowledge	53.5
Constructing paragraph headings	51.3
Relating parts of the text to one another	41.9
Constructing meaning and learning from pictures in the text	41.7

Source: Adapted from M.C. Wittrock and H.J. Schultze, "School and Classroom Evaluation." In H. Singer, R.B. Ruddell, J. McNeil, and M.C. Wittrock (Eds.), *Testing Achievement in Basic Skills* (Vol. 1). Final report, University of California, 1982. Adapted by permission.

In a recently completed study (Wittrock & Schultze, 1982) we obtained data from school systems in California indicating that teachers clearly want tests that measure the strategies students use to comprehend texts. Table 2.1 reports these data. Teachers do not get these diagnostically useful data from currently available tests of reading achievement.

Researchers also could use measures of student and teacher cognitive and affective processes to refine their models and to construct interpretations of how instruction influences achievement by stimulating student thought processes. In this way, the design and development of useful measures of cognitive and affective student and teacher thought processes promise basic and practical contributions to understanding the effects of teaching that lead to predictable improvements in instruction.

REFERENCES

AVOLIO, B.J., ALEXANDER, R.A., BARRETT, G.V., & STERNS, H.L. (1981) Designing a measure of visual selective attention to assess individual differences in information processing. *Applied Psychological Measurement, 5,* 29–42.
AU, K. (1977, December). *Cognitive training and reading achievement.* Paper presented at the meeting of the Association for the Advancement of Behavior Therapy, Atlanta, GA.
BELMONT, J.M. BUTTERFIELD, E.C., & FERRETTI, R.P. (1982). To secure transfer of training instruct self-management skills. In D.K. Detterman & R.J. Sternberg (Eds.) *How and how much can intelligence be increased.* Norwood, NJ: ABLEX.
BRANSFORD, J., SHERWOOD, R., VYE, N., & RIESER, J. (1986). Teaching thinking and problem solving. *American Psychologist, 41,* 1078–1089.
BROPHY, J.E. (1981). Teacher praise: A functional analysis. *Review of Educational Research, 5,* 5–32.

BROWN, A., CAMPIONE, J., & DAY, J.E. (1981). Learning to learn: On training students to learn from texts. *Educational Researcher, 10*(2), 14–21.

BROWN, J.S., & VANLEHN K. (1982). Towards a generative theory of "bugs." In T.P. Carpenter, J. Moser, & T. Romberg (Eds.), *Addition and subtraction: A developmental perspective* pp. 117–135. Hillsdale, NJ: Lawrence Erlbaum.

BUTTERFIELD, E.C., & BELMONT, J.M. (1977). Assessing and improving the executive cognitive functions of mentally retarded people. In I. Bialer & M. Sternlicht (Eds.), *The psychology of mental retardation* pp. 277–318. New York: Psychological Dimensions.

CAPELLI, C.A., & MARKMAN, E.M. (1982). Suggestions for training comprehension monitoring. *Topics in Learning and Learning Disabilities, 2,* 79–85.

DECHARMS, R. (1972). Personal causation training in the schools. *Journal of Applied Psychology, 2,* 95–113.

DOCTOROW, M.J., WITTROCK, M.C., & MARKS, C.B. (1978). Generative processes in reading comprehension. *Journal of Educational Psychology, 70,* 109–118.

DOUGLAS, V.I., PARRY, P., MARTIN, P., & GARSON, C. (1976). Assessment of a cognitive training program for hyperactive children. *Journal of Abnormal Child Psychology, 4,* 389–410.

DWECK, C. (1975). The role of expectations and attributions in the alleviation of learned helplessness. *Journal of Personality and Social Psychology, 31,* 674–685.

KEOGH, B.K., & GLOVER, A.T. (1980). The generality and durability of cognitive training effects. *Exceptional Education Quarterly, 1*(1), 75–81.

KEOGH, B.K., & HALL, R.J. (1984). Cognitive training with learning-disabled pupils. In A. Meyers and C.W. Craighead (Eds.), *Cognitive behavior therapy for children* (pp. 163–191).

LEFCOURT, H.M. (1982). *Locus of control: Current trends in theory and research.* Hillsdale, NJ: Lawrence Erlbaum.

LINDEN, M., & WITTROCK, M.C. (1981). The teaching of reading comprehension according to the model of generative learning. *Reading Research Quarterly, 17,* 44–57.

MALAMUTH, S. (1979). Self-management training for children with reading problems: Effects on reading performance and sustained attention. *Cognitive Therapy and Research, 4,* 279–289.

MCCOMBS, B.L. (1982). Transitioning learning strategies research into practice: Focus on the student in technical training. *Journal of Instructional Development, 5,* 10–17.

MCNEIL, J. (1987). *Reading comprehension: New directions for the classroom.* Glenview, IL: Scott Foresman.

MEICHENBAUM, D. (1981, April). *Teaching thinking: A cognitive behavioral approach.* Paper presented at the meeting of the Society for Learning Disabilities and Remedial Education, New York.

METALSKY, G.I., & ABRAMSON, L.Y. (1981). Attributional styles: Toward a framework for conceptualization and assessment. In P. Kendall & S. Hollon (Eds.), *Assessment strategies for cognitive-behavioral interventions* pp. 13–58. New York: Academic Press.

NAVEH-BENJAMIN, M., MCKEACHIE, W.J., LIN, Y., & TUCKER, D.G. (1986). Inferring students' cognitive structures and their development using the "Ordered Tree Technique." *Journal of Educational Psychology, 78,* 130–140.

OSBORNE, R.J., & WITTROCK, M.C. (1983). Learning science: A generative process. *Science Education, 67,* 489–508.

OSBORNE, R.J., & WITTROCK, M.C. (1985). The generative learning model and its implications for science education. *Studies in Science Education, 12,* 59–87.

PALINSCAR, A.S., & BROWN, A.L. (1984). Reciprocal teaching of comprehension-fostering and comprehension-monitoring activities. *Cognition and Instruction, 1,* 117–175.

PEARSON, P.D. (1985). *Handbook of reading research.* Newark, DE: International Reading Association.

PETERSON, P., & SWING, S. (1982). Beyond time on task: Students' reports of their thought processes during direct instruction. *Elementary School Journal, 82,* 481–491.

PIONTKOWSKI, D., & CALFEE, R. (1979). Attention in the classroom. In G. Hale & M. Lewis (Eds.), *Attention and cognitive development* pp. 297–329. New York: Plenum Press.

POSNER, M.I., & FRIEDRICH, F.J. (1986). Attention and the control of cognition. In S. Friedman, K. Klivington, & R. Peterson (Eds.), *The brain, cognition, and education* pp. 81–103. New York: Academic Press.

SHAVELSON, R.J. (1974). Some methods for examining content structure and cognitive structure in instruction. *Educational Psychologist, 11,* 110–122.

STERNBERG, R.J. (1981). Testing and cognitive psychology. *American Psychologist, 36,* 1181–1189.

WEINER, B. (1979). A theory of motivation for some classroom experiences. *Journal of Educational Psychology, 71,* 3–25.

WEINSTEIN, C., & MAYER, R. (1986). The teaching of learning strategies. In M. Wittrock (Ed.), *The handbook of research on teaching, (3rd ed.).* pp. 315–327. New York: Macmillan.

WITTROCK, M.C. (1974). Learning as a generative process. *Educational Psychologist, 11,* 87–95.

WITTROCK, M.C. (1978). The cognitive movement in instruction. *Educational Psychologist, 13,* 15–30.

WITTROCK, M.C. (1981). Reading comprehension. In F.J. Pirozzolo & M.C. Wittrock (Eds.), *Neuropsychological and cognitive processes in reading* pp. 219–259. New York: Academic Press.

WITTROCK, M.C. (1986a). Education and recent research on attention and knowledge acquisition. In S.L. Freidman, K.A. Klivington, & R.W. Peterson (Eds.), *The brain, cognition, and education* pp. 151–169. New York: Academic Press.

WITTROCK, M.C. (1986b). Students' thought processes. In M.C. Wittrock (Ed.), *Handbook of research on teaching (3rd ed.)* pp. 297–314. New York: Macmillan.

WITTROCK, M.C. (1987). Process-oriented measures of comprehension. *The Reading Teacher,* 734–737.

WITTROCK, M.C. (1990). Generative processes of comprehension *Educational Psychologist, 24,* 345–376.

WITTROCK, M.C., & ALESANDRINI, K. (in press) Generation of summaries and analogies and analytic and holistic abilities. *American Educational Research Journal.*

WITTROCK, M.C., & KELLY, R. (1984). *Teaching reading comprehension to adults in basic skills courses.* Final Report, University of California, Los Angeles, Graduate School of Education (Vols. 1–3).

WITTROCK, M.C., & LUMSDAINE, A.A. (1977). Instructional psychology. In M.R. Rosenzweig & L.W. Porter (Eds.), *Annual Review of Psychology, 28,* 417–459.

WITTROCK, M.C., & SCHULTZE, H.J. (1982). School and classroom evaluation. In H. Singer, R.B. Ruddell, J. McNeil, & M.C. Wittrock (Eds.), *Testing achievement in basic skills* (Vol. I, pp. 151–200). Final report, University of California.

THREE

EXPERTISE
AND ASSESSMENT

Robert Glaser

In Chapter 3, Robert Glaser discusses the implications of the cognitive analysis of performance for educational assessment. Studies of expertise have investigated the nature of the knowledge and cognitive processes that underlie developing competence in various domains of learning. These studies have shown that critical aspects of expert performance include: the organization of knowledge for quick retrieval from memory; the imposition of meaningful patterns in problem solving; the proceduralization of knowledge for problem solution; and the utilization of self-monitoring skills to secure effective performance. These findings on the character of expertise can serve as a basis for the integration of cognitive theory with psychometric techniques in the design of achievement tests that assess growing proficiency in subject-matter learning.

In 1963, the concept of criterion-referenced measurement emerged in work I was pursuing to encourage the development of procedures for assessing the outcomes of learning; the aim was to envision assessments of proficiency that could be referenced to progressive states of competence. (Glaser & Klaus, 1962; Glaser, 1963). The weak link in the construction of proficiency tests was our descriptions of the performances to be measured; systematic techniques were needed to describe more adequately the components of proficiency at specified levels of competence. My thinking drew on the then-prevalent theory of learning and instruction, because criterion-referenced measurement is dependent on some analytic account of human performances and the objectives of learning.

In the ensuing years, developments in psychometric theory have significantly influenced testing techniques. There have also been significant changes in the theories that guide our understanding of competence in areas of complex knowledge and skills. The task now, in large part, is to examine our new understanding to relate these advances.

The assessment systems we derive depend intimately on our knowledge of how humans learn and acquire knowledge and skill; research and development take their cues from findings about the nature of human performance. In the present state of the art, the study of performance must be given precedence over or, at the least, equal status with measurement technique for effective approaches to subject-matter assessment. A scientific base for instruction and the assessment of its outcomes cannot prosper if we have only minimal understanding of the characteristics of acquired performances. These characteristics must be described so that the changes that take place with learning can be specified. Thus, the study of the knowledge structures and processes entailed in human competence and expertise is an essential focus for determining dimensions of assessment.

STUDIES OF EXPERTISE

The seeds of the study of expert performance were sown in the fertile ground of Newell and Simon's 1972 *Human Problem Solving*. The theory they were developing was content and knowledge oriented, and they speculated: "If content is a substantial determinant of human behavior—if, in fact, the message is a lot more message than medium—then information-processing theories have opportunities for describing human behavior veridically that are foreclosed to theories unable to cope with content" (p. 11). Content

This article is a revision of the author's address at the UCLA Conference on Approaches to Subject Matter Assessment, December 1987. Preparation of this article was sponsored in part by the Center for the Study of Learning (CSL) at the Learning Research and Development Center of the University of Pittsburgh. CSL is funded by the Office of Educational Research and Improvement of the U.S. Department of Education.

structures are determinants, to a large extent, of the power of cognitive process in competent performance.

Newell and Simon further pointed out that, with emerging theories, a standard approach is to study the steady-state operations of a system, where changes are not salient. Thus, their tactic for scientific investigation was to explore asymptotic behavior—what happens in the long run. In studies of competent performance and expertise, the objective of investigation is to give an articulated account of a performance that has developed over time, through learning and experience, to describe invariant and content-specific properties that characterize highly competent processing.

In the Newell and Simon chapter on chess that refers to the work of de Groot (1965), we find lines of thought that anticipate the now consistent findings about the nature of expertise. In attempting to find measures to distinguish strong from weaker players, de Groot was unsuccessful with statistical assessments of search and analysis. He finally succeeded in separating strong from weak players by using perceptual tests requiring recall of chess positions after a very brief exposure to them. Chess experts reproduced the positions perfectly, but weaker players recalled them only partially and sometimes incorrectly. De Groot proposed that perceptual abilities fostered by extensive chess knowledge were characteristic of highly competent players. He also found that, for strong players, particular board features suggested move possibilities in a highly automatic way; they decided on moves without any verbalized problem solving, that is, almost intuitively. "Exposed to a new position," Newell and Simon observed, "a skilled human player does not appear to engage in a search of move sequences. Instead, he appears to be occupied with perceiving the essential properties of the position. . . . There is clear evidence that this first act of definition differs substantially from all others" (p. 761). In this observation we can see the beginnings of a characterization of highly competent expert performance. Humans, in general, when first presented with a problem, must recognize or understand it in some way; either the problem space must be constructed, or evoked if one already exists in memory. Experts perform this phase of problem solving in a particular fashion—with notable insight.

To understand the chess master's pattern recognition superiority, Chase and Simon (1973) attempted to uncover structures of chess knowledge that masters possessed and to trace knowledge's impact on performance. It appeared that both masters and novices recalled the chess positions in chunks that reproduce positions pattern by pattern: Stereotypic patterns that chess players see frequently become connected through experience. The difference between the novice and expert chess players' performances was the size of the chunks they drew on as they played. The novices' chunks involved possible moves for single pieces; the masters' involved configurations of pieces and were larger. The novice and the master recalled about the same number of chunks but the experts' chunks revealed familiarity with diverse intricate patterns and pattern sequences. It was estimated that a chess master is able to recognize about 50,000 configurations of chess pieces, an amount nearly as large as the number of words a fluent reader recognizes.

Organized Knowledge

Study of expert/novice differences in other domains has continued to reveal the impact of knowledge on pattern recognition. For example, in electronics (Egan & Schwartz, 1979), skilled technicians reconstructing symbolic drawings of circuit diagrams do so according to the functional nature of the elements in the circuit, such as amplifiers, rectifiers, and filters. Novice technicians, however, reproduce the circuits based on the spatial proximity of the elements; the chunks they draw on do not accommodate knowledge of function. In radiological diagnosis, experts organize the cues in x-ray plates by imposing schemata that are rich in diagnostic and anatomical information, and they refine these schemata as various hypotheses and related evidence are obtained. Novices are less flexible in generating specialized schemata from their initial representation of the cues in the x-ray (Lesgold, 1984).

Problem representation is a profound aspect of expert performance. The generation of a "deep structure" representation is characteristic of experts (Chi, Feltovich, & Glaser, 1981; Chi, Glaser, & Rees, 1982). Experts learn to induce implicit principles from the given features of problems, and they represent problems in terms of these principles. When novice and expert physicists are asked to classify a set of problems, they approach the task on entirely different bases. The novices work from surface features, grouping rotation problems, inclined plane problems, or spring problems, to develop their classifications. In contrast, the experts group problems that are quite dissimilar on the surface as the conservation of energy or Newton's Second Law problems. The experts map surface features of the problem onto these deeper principles. And these principles are more predictive of the method of solution.

Like the chess results, the evidence accumulated over the past 15 years shows that experts in many domains are able to remember information extremely rapidly, in chunks, organizations, and meaningful patterns of knowledge, and so have access to associated sequences of moves and procedures. The similarity between pattern recognition in playing chess, reconstructing circuit diagrams, interpreting x-rays, or solving problems in physics and mathematics, is that the functional properties or "meaningful deep structures" are rapidly perceived by experts, whereas surface features and literal descriptive aspects guide the thinking of less-than-expert individuals.

The results of converging findings to date suggest that at least two aspects of performance reflect the influence of rich knowledge structures. Experts, as I have indicated, have a great deal of domain-specific information, and this information is highly organized and conceptually integrated. Organized knowledge appears to account for the rapid pattern recognition and categorization apparent in performance. Moreover, experts use their knowledge in reasoning—qualitative as well as quantitative reasoning—with notable facility. The expert readily makes causal inferences about a system model prior to applying any quantitative procedures, calculations, or specific solution routines and then displays unusual efficiency in such application.

Reasoning Abilities

In the solution of elementary physics problems, differences in qualitative as well as quantitative reasoning distinguish experts' from novices' performances. Two disparities are easily noted. The most obvious is time-to-solution, the speed with which a problem is solved. The skill of the individual determines how rapidly a solution is achieved (Simon & Simon, 1978; Larkin, 1981). Experts are generally more efficient in searching and representing their solution space and, as a result, may perform four times faster than novices when tackling standard physics problems. Moreover, their pause times between retrieving successive equations or groups of equations are abbreviated by comparison to novices'. Experts appear to group their equations in chunks, so that eliciting one equation activates related equations, which are retrieved rapidly. It appears that, for experts, physics equations are stored in related configurations; accessing one principle leads to accessing another (Larkin, 1979).

The issue of time-to-solution is not straightforward. In the initial phase of problem solving, expert physicists appear to devote significant time to "qualitative analysis" (Larkin, 1977; Larkin, 1980; Larkin, McDermott, Simon, & Simon, 1980) in which they display "physical intuition" (Simon & Simon, 1978). Prior to retrieval of equations, prior to actual problem solving, experts reflect for a disproportionate amount of time on the nature of a problem, whereas novices plunge in immediately with calculations. This beginning phase of problem solving has been the object of empirical and theoretical analysis and continues to play a key role in the investigation of the impact of knowledge on expert performance.

In various domains, qualitative analysis involves representation of the problem in terms of a real-world runnable model. Facility with model building is another evidence of experts' superior reasoning ability. For example, when algebra word problems involving boards of different lengths that correspond to physically unrealizable situations were presented to students, a few of them perceived the "incongruity" in the problems (Paige & Simon, 1966). In contrast, other students proceeded to evoke equations before realizing that the solutions would be meaningless (e.g., a negative quantity for the length of a board). The former, more adept solvers apparently represented the problem more reflectively, so that the physical dimensions of the boards were clear to them, although they had made no calculations.

In physics problem solving, the construction of a physical model provides a basis for checking errors. The physical model, developed as part of the problem representation, provides a global description of important features of the problem situation, and it permits inferences to be drawn about objects and their relations that go beyond the problem statement. For example, in a statics problem involving a ladder leaning against a wall, the model would include the ladder, the floor, the wall, the points of contact, and forces operating, as well as gravity.

Cognitive Development

The focus on knowledge structures in studies of expertise has become increasingly prevalent in developmental studies as well (Carey, 1985; Siegler, 1978; Keil, 1984). The cognitive changes entailed in accruing competence occur in children as their knowledge structures become more complete, differentiated, or articulated. Explanation of developmental changes in terms of knowledge differentiation and integration has at least equal power to the postulation of the maturation of general learning processes (Keil, 1984).

The work of Chi (1978) has shown that many supposed stage-like changes in general memory-processing ability are heavily dependent on the degree of expertise that children have in the conceptual domain being tested. In studies contrasting the knowledge structures of expert/novice children in the domain of biology several conclusions have been drawn that are consistent with previous expert/novice research with adults (Gobbo & Chi, 1986). In classifying plants or animals, novice children tended to focus on the explicit surface features of a phenomenon, whereas experts focused on the implicit or "deep level" concepts. And the frequency of verbalized "implicit" information about various species was much greater in the expert than the novice children. Moreover, the expert child's knowledge was more structured, more integrated and cohesive. Experts' protocols were connected syntactically, producing the form of a more coherent discourse than novices'. In experts, the generation of one piece of information activated other associated knowledge. This suggests an associative network from which causal inferences about class membership and predictions about the features of new examples of a species or kind could be made. As a consequence of its integration in a network, expert children used their knowledge in a more sophisticated and accessible way. They showed a higher frequency of semantic comparisons through analogical reasoning and could reason from both the presence or absence of a feature, whereas novices tended to be able to infer only on the basis of the presence of certain features. Overall, the more structured and cohesive knowledge in expert children facilitated their access to and use of their knowledge in more developmentally mature ways than novice children of the same age.

Summary Comment

These accrued findings on the nature of human expertise and development give enhanced meaning to the concept of criterion-referenced assessment. Consider the following generalizations:

1. The precision of expert performance results from specialized schemata that drive performance. Expertise in one domain is no guarantee of expertise in others. Specificity of performance is evidenced by the fact that expert proficiency can be disrupted by the presentation of random (or meaningless) patterns or poorly structured problems. Under such conditions, experts lose their rapid perceptual and representational ability and resort to general problem-solving strategies.

2. Experts develop the ability to perceive large meaningful patterns. Pattern recognition occurs so rapidly that it appears to take on the character of "intuitions." In contrast, the patterns novices recognize are smaller, less articulated, more literal and surface oriented, and much less related to inferences and abstracted principles. As pointed out, the extraordinary representational ability of experts appears to depend on the organization of knowledge existing in memory.

3. The fast-access pattern recognition and representational capability of experts facilitate problem perception in a way that reduces the role of memory search and general processing. By contrast, novices display a good deal of search and processing of a general nature. Although it can be assumed that experts and novices have similar capacities for cognitive processing, the outstanding performance of experts derives primarily from how their knowledge is structured for retrieval, pattern recognition, and inference.

4. The knowledge of experts is highly procedural and goal oriented. Concepts are bound to procedures for their application and to conditions under which these procedures are useful. The functional knowledge of experts is related strongly to their knowledge of the goal structure of a problem. Experts and novices may be equally competent at recalling small specific items of domain-related information. But high-knowledge individuals are much better at relating these items in cause-and-effect sequences that enable the pursuit of goals and subgoals of problem solution.

5. The experience of experts enables them to develop skilled self-regulatory processes. These cognitive skills are manifested by proficiency in techniques of solution monitoring, by the allocation of attention, and by sensitivity to informational feedback. Self-regulatory processes are sometimes evidenced by the fact that experts may be slower than novices in initially encoding a difficult problem, but are faster problem solvers overall.

WRITING SKILL

Now let me speculate about expertise in writing in terms of the generalizations I have just offered. Issues of domain specificity, knowledge and process, representation, task sensitivity, and goal orientation take interesting shapes when the performance in question is writing in academic domains.

Specificity

The specificity of writing expertise is emphasized by David Bartholomae, who holds that, "Everytime a student sits down to write for us, he has to invent the university for the occasion—invent the university, that is, or a branch of it, like History, or Anthropology, or Economics, or English. He has to learn to speak our language, to speak as we do, to try on the peculiar ways of knowing, selecting, evaluating, reporting, concluding, and arguing that define the discourse of our community." Further, he says a student must learn "to work within fields where the rules governing the presentation of example or the development of an argument are both distinct and, even to a professional, mysterious" (Bartholomae, 1985).

Bartholomae points out that although in introductory writing courses the student is concerned with university discourse in its most generalized form, competence in writing, in the longer term, requires that students locate themselves in disciplinary forms of discourse that are not immediately theirs. He adds that students who can write reasonably correct narratives in one domain may be unable to grapple with assignments in unfamiliar domains— the floundering is not unlike that manifested by experts when they are required to operate outside of their disciplines.

Knowledge and Process

Identifiable declarative and procedural knowledge is needed for competent writing performances. Novice writers are not necessarily inept thinkers; they are usually simply unfamiliar with the knowledge base needed as building blocks of a discussion and with the conventions and techniques of expository discourse. The patterns of reasoning that we expect in academic writing are not inherent in our thinking, but are conventional, learnable forms of academic argumentation and rhetoric that have been shaped to carry key concepts and facts. For example, in addition to the syntactic conventions of language, academic writers must learn to support and make clear the generalizations upon which their arguments hinge. As novices, they may not be aware that examples and illustrations should be tied to generalizations with statements that explicitly explain their relevance. Competent writing involves acquiring this conventional technique. Another strategy to be acquired is defining and responding to an audience. These forms of writing knowledge comprise the knowledge structures acquired by writers who develop reasonable proficiency.

Representation

Research on writing skill (particularly as described by Flower, Hayes, Carey, Schriver, and Stratman, 1986), like expert and novice studies, demonstrates that the initial representation of a task is highly influential. Revision is a critical task in all formal written discourse, and students' representations of problems and opportunities in what they have written determine the nature of subsequent revision. Their search through their own texts can be of a local and shallow or of a global and more meaningful nature. Consequently, inexperienced and experienced writers make different kinds of changes in the course of revision. Novices typically spend little time on rereading a draft and focus on the conventions and rules of writing, using deletion and addition as important strategies (Bridwell, 1980). Experienced writers generate several successive drafts and conceptualize the task as holistic, involving changes in content, structure, and voice, and make many more changes that affect the text's meaning, manifesting deeper representations of the problems they have identified and the tactics for solution.

Representation of the tasks of revision is apparently accomplished in one of two ways—either by a monitoring and evaluation process, which builds up a problem representation that carries with it information and strategies for solving the problem, or by a more immediate categorization or pattern-recognition process that recurs as the text is being read. In the first case (Flower, Hayes, Carey, Schriver, & Stratman, 1986), experienced writers constantly monitor their progress; they observe the features of their text, apply the alternative writing strategies in their repertoires, and focus on an appropriate goal. The task representation reflects this interplay between the writer's analysis of text features and the writer's store of knowledge about revision strategies and currently attainable goals.

Alternatively, problem representation can result from rapid categorization of faults in a text. Like the experts in other areas, the good writer has a repertoire of patterns that are quickly recognized; this rapid pattern recognition brings forth the strategies and applicable goals, just as board patterns do for chess masters and x-ray patterns do for expert radiologists. A proficient writer has a rich store of interrelated knowledge and employs problem classifications that go beyond comma faults or noun-verb disagreements to deeper structures, such as poor uses of metaphor or inept use of quotes or paraphrases. This rapid categorization of problems takes on the character of intuitive performance in writing as well as in other fields.

Task Sensitivity and Goal Orientation

In carrying out revision, competent writers show a significant sensitivity to task demands and to goals. They seize and take advantage of opportunities they uncover in the text to improve the quality of their performance. Again, this is typical of the task and feature sensitivity of the expert performer in other fields. Depending upon the skill of the writer and the difficulty of the task, the representation that is generated can entail well- or poorly defined goals. Revisions can be instituted that are momentarily too global to attain and are underconstrained, or are too constrained and overly simple. Inexperienced writers may build a representation quickly because their knowledge is less complex, they have fewer strategies at their command, and their subgoal analysis is superficial, with the result that the range of changes appropriate to the text are never addressed, though the need for them may be recognized. Experts, by contrast, choose global goals or subgoals, depending upon the state of the current draft, sometimes focusing on a subtask so that a more complex goal can be pursued later. They adapt successive passes, so that appropriate ranges of revision are accomplished.

Writing expertise probably ranges along a continuum from routine or conventional expertise to adaptive expertise. Routine experts excel in speed, accuracy, and automaticity of performance; they construct mental models convenient and efficient for performing standard tasks, but they are seldom innovative and they lack adaptability when faced with new kinds of problems. Probably, repeated application of a procedure, with little variation, leads to routine expertise. Adaptive expertise requires variation and is encouraged by playful situations and educational settings where understanding and transfer are valued along with efficient performance (Hatano & Inagaki, 1983).

INDICATORS OF DEVELOPING COMPETENCE

Essential characteristics of proficient performance have been described in various domains and these provide useful indices for assessment. We know that, at specific stages of learning, there exist different integrations of knowledge, different forms of skill, differences in access to knowledge, and differences in the efficiency of performance. These stages can define criteria for test design. We can now propose a set of candidate dimensions along which subject-matter competence can be assessed. As competence in a subject matter grows, evidence of a knowledge base that is increasingly *coherent, principled, useful,* and *goal-oriented* is displayed, and test items can be designed to capture such evidence.

The Coherence of Knowledge

As competence is attained, elements of knowledge become increasingly interconnected so that proficient individuals access coherent chunks rather than fragments of information. Beginners' knowledge is spotty, consisting of isolated definitions and superficial understandings. As proficiency develops, these items of information become structured and are integrated with past organizations of knowledge so that they are retrieved in larger units from memory. Thus, structuredness, coherence, and accessibility to interrelated chunks of knowledge become targets for assessment.

Principled Problem Solving

Certain forms of problem interpretation are correlated with the ability to carry out the details of a task or the steps of a problem solution. Novices work on the basis of the surface features of a task situation or problem; in contrast, more proficient individuals identify principles that lie beneath apparent surface features. An ability to recognize underlying principles and patterns is an indication of developing competence that could be assessed by appropriate test tasks in verbal and graphic situations.

Usable Knowledge

Studies of expert/novice differences suggest that the course of knowledge acquisition proceeds from the accumulation of facts in declarative or propositional form to their compilation in condition-action form. Novices can know a principle or a rule or a specialized vocabulary without knowing the conditions where that knowledge applies and how it can be used most effectively. When experts access their knowledge, it is bound to conditions of applicability. Experts and novices may be equally competent at recalling specific items of information, but the experts relate these items to the goals of problem solution and conditions for action. The progression from declarative to procedural and goal-oriented information is a significant dimension for assessment of competence in an area of knowledge.

Self-Regulatory Skills

Competent people develop skills for monitoring their performances. They rapidly check the appropriateness of their problem-solving tactics, and they are more accurate at judging problem difficulty. They are able to apportion their time, ask questions about what they have to do, assess the relevance of their knowledge, and predict the outcomes of their performance. These self-regulatory skills vary and are less developed in individuals who have insufficient knowledge to anticipate task requirements. Where they are well developed, they enhance knowledge because they oversee its use. Self-regulatory skills are important candidates for assessment and instruction, and they can be significant predictors of an individual's problem-solving abilities.

CONCLUSION

Given the growing body of information about human competence and performance, the emphasis in theories of learning has shifted from the accumulation of facts and their reinforcement, to the structure and coherence of knowledge and its accessibility in problem solving and reasoning. Cognitive studies investigate how knowledge is organized, how problems are represented for solution, how mental models are imposed on the interpretation of information, and how competence in a subject matter develops when the acquisition of facts and propositions is heightened with their flexible use under varied conditions. The analysis of performance is making explicit outcomes of learning and experience that can be assessed to guide the further acquisition of knowledge and skill in various domains. We are better able now to describe the stages of competence or levels of achievement that underlie the progressions of learning within a domain of knowledge and, as a result, can more effectively foster the transition between levels of competence by the design of appropriate instruction.

Given the growth of the research base for test design, we should be in a position to consider cognitive-psychological theory as well as psychometric theory in the design of tests. To date, we have been reaping the benefits of psychometrics, employing advances in statistical theory, but have had less opportunity to emphasize the cognitive and developmental theory that explicates human thinking and performance. Given this state of knowledge, most of the work of testing technology—the analysis of item difficulty, discrimination indices, scaling and norming procedures, and the analysis of factorial composition—has occurred after test items were constructed. In the future, test design will entail extensive attention to theory before and during item design as well. If we are to reap the benefits of research on human performance and development, we must rely on the emerging picture of the properties of acquired proficiency in school subjects to make tests responsive to the structures and processes that develop as individuals move from beginning to advanced learners. Thus, the assessment of achievement can be more closely tied to our understanding of progressions in learning and the accrual of results of effective teaching.

In closing, let me note that, to place tests in the service of learning in a marriage of cognitive and psychometric theory, we must consider assessment of school subject matters as measures of skills and dispositions that are essential to further learning. Once mastered, the skills and knowledge of a domain can become enabling competencies for the future. Keeping this in mind, we must measure student attainment in a way that takes into account, for example, that the purpose of learning to write is to enable further learning. Addressing writing as an enabling skill implies a particular environment for achievement, whereby the command of grammar and syntax becomes sufficient to allow the student to concentrate on analyzing or inter-preting a topic and to observe the conventions of the domain. Writing, as an enabling skill, provides a way of organizing as well as communicating thought. Those who cannot express thoughts in writing are clearly at a great disadvantage, in both work and school, so that the standard of assessment here should involve the ability to use writing to help clarify ideas and build persuasive arguments. Much the same can be said about other school subject matters, including the sciences. We must assess the ability to think critically about our social and physical world. Knowledge at every level should be assessed in ways that allow students to see how they can use it to gather further information, evaluate evidence, weigh alternative courses for action, and articulate reasoned arguments. We should measure students' ability to question statements others present, as well as their own views. This concern with enablement raises the level of competence that we should expect of students and for which schools should be held accountable.

REFERENCES

BARTHOLOMAE, D. (1985). Inventing the university. In M. Rose (Ed.), *When a writer can't write: Studies in writer's block and other composing process problems* (pp. 134–166). New York: Guilford.
BRIDWELL, L.S. (1980). Revising strategies in twelfth grade students' transactional writing. *Research in the Teaching of English, 14*(3), 107–122.
CAREY, S. (1985). *Conceptual change in childhood.* Cambridge, MA: MIT Press.
CHASE, W.G., & SIMON, H.A. (1973). Perception in chess. *Cognitive Science, 4,* 55–81.
CHI, M.T.H. (1978). Knowledge structures and memory development. In R. Siegler (Ed.), *Children's thinking: What develops?* (pp. 73–96). Hillsdale, NJ: Lawrence Erlbaum.
CHI, M.T.H., FELTOVICH, P., & GLASER, R. (1981). Categorization and representation of physics problems by experts and novices. *Cognitive Science, 5,* 121–152.
CHI, M.T.H., GLASER, R., & REES, E. (1982). Expertise in problem solving. In R. Sternberg (Ed.), *Advances in the psychology of human intelligence* (pp. 7–70). Hillsdale, NJ: Lawrence Erlbaum.
DEGROOT, A.D. (1965). *Thought and choice in chess.* The Hague, Netherlands: Mouton.
EGAN, D.E., & SCHWARTZ, B.J. (1979). Chunking in recalling symbolic drawings. *Memory and Cognition, 7,* 149–158.
FLOWER, L.S., HAYES, J.R., CAREY, L., SCHRIVER, K., & STRATMAN, J. (1986). Detection, diagnosis, and the strategies of revision. *College Composition and Communication, 37*(1), 16–55.
GLASER, R. (1963). Instructional technology and the measurement of learning outcomes: Some questions. *American Psychologist, 18,* 519–521.
GLASER, R., & KLAUS, D.J. (1962). Proficiency measurement: Assessing human performance. In R.M. Gagne (Ed.), *Psychological principles in system development* (pp. 419–474). New York: Holt, Rinehart & Winston.
GOBBO, C., & CHI, M.T.H. (1986). How knowledge is structured and used by expert and novice children. *Cognitive Development, 1,* 221–237.
HATANO, G., & INAGAKI, K. (1983). *Two courses of expertise.* Paper presented at the Conference on Child Development in Japan and the United States, Stanford, CA.
KEIL, F.C. (1984). Mechanisms in cognitive development and the structure of knowledge. In R.J. Sternberg (Ed.), *Mechanisms of cognitive development* (pp. 81–100). New York: Freeman.

LARKIN, J.H. (1977). *Problem solving in physics* (Technical Report). Berkeley, CA: University of California, Group in Science and Mathematics Education.

LARKIN, J.H. (1979). Processing information for effective problem solving. *Engineering Education,* 70(3), 285-288.

LARKIN, J.H. (1980). *Understanding, problem representations, and skill in physics.* Paper presented at NIE-LRDC Conference on Thinking and Learning Skills, Pittsburgh, PA.

LARKIN, J.H., McDERMOTT, J., SIMON, D.P., & SIMON, H.A. (1980). Models of competence in solving physics problems. *Cognitive Science, 4,* 317-345.

LARKIN, J.H. (1981). Enriching formal knowledge: A model for learning to solve textbook physics problems. In J. Anderson (Ed.), *Cognitive skills and their acquisition* (pp. 311-334). Hillsdale, NJ: Lawrence Erlbaum.

LESGOLD, A.M. (1984). Acquiring expertise. In J.P. Anderson & S.M. Kosslyn (Eds.), *Tutorials in learning and memory: Essays in honor of Gordon Bower* (pp. 31-60). New York: Freeman.

NEWELL, A., & SIMON, H.A. (1972). *Human problem solving.* Englewood Cliffs, NJ: Prentice-Hall.

PAIGE, J.M., & SIMON, H.A. (1966). Cognitive processes in solving algebra word problems. In B. Kleinmutz (Ed.), *Problem solving* (pp. 51-119). New York: Wiley.

SIEGLER, R.S. (1978). The origins of scientific reasoning. In R.S. Siegler (Ed.), *Children's thinking: What develops?* (pp. 109-149). Hillsdale, NJ: Lawrence Erlbaum.

SIMON, D.P., & SIMON, H.A. (1978). Individual differences in solving physics problems. *Cognitive Science, 4,* 317-345.

FOUR

TOWARD BETTER INTELLIGENCE TESTS

Robert J. Sternberg

In Chapter 4, Robert J. Sternberg presents a provocative model of intelligent thinking that leads to several fundamental implications for the improvement of the testing of intelligence. His triarchic model of human intelligence consists of a componential subtheory, an experiential subtheory, and a contextual subtheory. The componential subtheory states how intelligence relates to one's inner world through three types of processes. First are the metacomponents, or executive planning, monitoring, and evaluation processes. Second are the performance components, which one uses to carry out the instructions of the executive processes. Third are the knowledge-acquisition components, which one uses to learn, to comprehend, and to remember information. The experiential subtheory relates intelligence to experience; and the contextual subtheory relates intelligence to the external world of the individual. Within this framework, he presents suggestions for revising and improving tests of human intelligence, such as measuring acquired knowledge separately from the ability to acquire that knowledge, measuring synthetic thinking, automatization, and applications of intelligence to everyday contexts.

We can do better. This is the main message of this essay on the form and content of the intelligence tests of the future. The future can be now. There is no reason to wait. We have the theory, the technology, and the motivation to do better. We can do it; we should do it.

The tests we have now aren't terrible, or even bad. As technological innovations go in psychology, they are about as good as we have gotten. Yet, with some modifications of and additions to what we have, we could have tests that are better. What forms would these modifications and additions take? Using my triarchic theory of human intelligence (Sternberg, 1985) as a basis for change, I think there are nine changes we could make right now, and one we could make in the near future, that would make for better tests. I describe each of the three aspects of the theory briefly and, concurrently, elaborate on the ten changes that I believe we should make. I then discuss the concrete implications of these changes for future research and testing practice.

THE TRIARCHIC MODEL

The Componential Subtheory

The componential subtheory of the triarchic theory specifies the relation between intelligence and the internal world: What are the mental processes, strategies, and representations that underlie intelligent thinking? According to the componential subtheory, the components of intelligence can be conveniently classified as being of three types: (1) metacomponents, or executive processes used to plan, monitor, and evaluate one's problem solving; (2) performance components, or nonexecutive processes used to implement the instructions of the metacomponents; and (3) knowledge-acquisition components, or nonexecutive processes used to learn how to solve problems in the first place.

Metacomponents   Intelligence tests should place greater emphasis upon metacomponential functioning. Current intelligence tests place relatively little emphasis upon metacomponential functioning. The emphasis of the tests, for example, is upon problem solving rather than upon problem finding, and upon solving problems quickly rather than upon knowing when to solve them quickly and when not to.

1. *Tests should place more emphasis upon recognizing and defining problems.* Test problems are given to students. They are usually well defined, fairly routine, unmotivating, and easily classifiable into types. But few problems in life, or even serious problems in schooling, have any of these characteristics. Perhaps the biggest stumbling block people face is knowing when

they even have a problem in the first place. Is the situation confronting them problematical, or is it essentially acceptable? Detroit did not know it had a problem with gas guzzlers until much too late—when the Japanese automobile companies had cornered the small-car market. What, exactly, is the problem that confronts one? In the Rex Stout novel, *Gambit*, Nero Wolfe is able to solve a puzzling murder only after he realizes that the murder was committed not to rid the murderer of the murder victim, but to rid the murderer of the individual whom he framed for the murder. Young assistant professors at Yale tend to rush to publish lots of articles in order to get promoted, rather than to concern themselves with the impact upon the field that those articles they have published are likely to have. Yet, it is impact rather than numbers that matters for promotion. The most important steps in dealing with problems are recognizing them and defining them; tests essentially bypass these important steps.

2. *Tests should place more emphasis upon resource allocation rather than resource utilization.* The overwhelming majority of group intelligence tests are timed. In order to do well, the individual has to be quite fast as well as quite accurate. Indeed, certain problems in school and in life require very rapid solution. But the large majority don't. When a student has multiple papers to write as well as multiple exams to study for, perhaps his or her hardest decision is how to allocate time. The smart move is not to write all the papers quickly or to study quickly for all of the exams, but to decide which papers to write quickly and which to spend more time on, and to decide just how long to allocate to studying for each exam. Later on, in careers, one's problem is not that everything has to be done quickly, but that only some things are worth spending time on, and others not. The trick is to decide which are which. Thus, resource allocation is at least as important as resource utilization, but the tests are much more oriented toward measuring the latter than the former.

Performance components

3. *More emphasis should be placed upon separating measurement of performance components from knowledge.* Consider a test such as the SAT verbal. What does a relatively poor showing on the verbal analogies subsection mean? It could mean that the student does not know the meanings of the relatively difficult words, or that the student knows the words, but is unable to reason with them. These two meanings have quite different implications both for understanding the intellectual functioning of the student and for remediating that student's functioning. Similarly, on the SAT Math, failure to solve certain algebra or geometry problems may represent either a lack of knowledge, a lack of reasoning ability, or both. Using the techniques of componential analysis (Sternberg, 1977) and related techniques, it is possible to obtain at least some differentiation between knowledge-based and reasoning-based performance.

4. *More emphasis should be placed upon separating measurement of performance components from each other.* Our measures currently give us only global and holistic assessment of performance componential functioning. But it is important to know which performance components are deficient (or not). For example, failure to transfer known principles to a given problem has a different meaning from success in transfer combined with failure in being able to use the principles in the given problem. Again, componential methodologies can assist in task decomposition and enable the examiner to discover the locus of success or failure.

Knowledge-acquisition components

5. *More separation is needed in the measurement of intelligence between acquired knowledge and the ability to acquire that knowledge.* Recent cognitive-psychological research shows the importance of knowledge in intelligent performance (see Chi, Glaser, & Rees, 1982) and that high performance on intelligence tests requires a substantial knowledge base. On the one hand, it is important to assess knowledge, given its importance in intelligent functioning. On the other hand, it is important to separate the ability to acquire knowledge from the knowledge itself. Current tests do not always do so in a compelling way. For example, synonyms tests, as well as antonyms tests such as those found on the Verbal SAT, largely measure knowledge. For the middle- to upper-middle-class child who has had plentiful exposure to verbal materials, such tests may serve as reasonable proxies for the ability to acquire such knowledge. But for children who have not had plentiful exposure, lack of opportunities to learn may result in acquired knowledge not adequately reflecting ability to acquire knowledge. For such students, tests that measure acquisition of knowledge at time of test may be more informative than tests that primarily measure how much knowledge has already been acquired. Our learning-for-context tests tap learning skills directly, rather than indirectly, as in the case of vocabulary tests (see Sternberg & Powell, 1983).

The Experiential Subtheory

The experiential subtheory deals with the relation of intelligence to experience. According to this subtheory, the components of intelligence best measure intelligence when they are (1) applied to relatively novel tasks or situations, or (2) in the process of becoming automatized. Extremely novel tasks are not useful for measuring intelligence, because the individual does not have sufficient experience to bring to bear upon them for his or her intelligence even to show through. Extremely familiar tasks are likely already to have become automatized, and performance on them may reflect differential past practice rather than differential intellectual functioning. The experiential subtheory suggests three implications for changes in testing.

6. *Intelligence tests should show increased emphasis upon synthetic thinking and relatively less emphasis upon analytic thinking.* At present, there is a

fairly gross imbalance in existing tests between measurement of analytic and synthetic thinking. There is far more emphasis on the latter than on the former. The tests measure well a person's ability to analyze ideas, but essentially do not measure at all the person's ability to come up with, or synthesize, ideas. Yet, whether in writing papers, designing research projects, or creating original artwork, synthetic ability is at least as important as analytic ability. In many occupations, the quality of one's ideas is more important than one's ability to analyze ideas, although of course one needs some critical ability to distinguish one's better ideas from one's poorer ones. In my own observations of both undergraduate and graduate students, I have become convinced that we select at Yale students who have shown excellent analytic abilities, but no particular synthetic abilities. Our students are better at criticizing the ideas of others than at inventing good new ideas of their own.

7. *Intelligence tests should show increased emphasis upon the measurement of insightful thinking.* On the mathematical portion of the SAT, there are a few problems that measure insightful problem solving, and are consciously labeled as such. Aside from these items, there is practically no need for insight abilities to attain a high score on the SAT. Performance on a typical intelligence test may require no insight abilities at all. Yet, much of the very best thinking that students and nonstudents alike do is insightful, and many of the major discoveries and inventions in the world are based upon insights. Moreover, the triarchic theory suggests that insightful thinking is a particularly important part of what distinguishes the intellectually gifted from the intellectually typical individual (Sternberg & Davidson, 1983). The balance between insightful and noninsightful thinking on intelligence tests should be shifted more in favor of the former.

8. *Intelligence tests ought to measure rate and asymptote of automatization directly.* The work of Hunt (1978) and others indicates that automatization of information is currently measured indirectly on verbal ability tests. In particular, higher performance, especially on verbal tests, is associated with more rapid and, hence, probably more automatized access of lexical information from long-term memory. In general, speed of information processing can be a weak proxy for asymptote of automatization. According to the triarchic theory, though, speed is only a proxy, not the psychological construct one wishes directly to measure. Moreover, none of the existing tests measure the rate at which automatization takes place. Because so many aspects of intellectual functioning, particularly in expert performance, are automatized, measuring rate and asymptote of automatization should be important aspects of a battery to measure intelligence.

The Contextual Subtheory

The contextual subtheory deals with the relation between intelligence and the external world of the individual. How does the context in which one lives affect what is considered to be intelligent behavior, and how well does the individual apply his or her intelligence in that context? All of us know individuals whose test performance is excellent, but whose ability to apply their intellect in everyday situations is notably deficient. We also know individuals showing the reverse pattern of test versus everyday performance.

According to the contextual subtheory, application of intelligence to context is through the service of three functions of intelligent behavior: adaptation to existing environments, shaping of existing environments so as to render them new environments, and selection of new environments. The subtheory has at least two important implications for intelligence testing.

9. *We need to emphasize more the application of intellectual skills in adaptation to everyday contexts.* Psychologists have shown repeatedly how difficult it is to get transfer of training. Transfer of intelligence is nontrivial as well. The same individual who may be keen at spotting contradictions in text or hidden assumptions in academic discourse may be a complete sucker for the most blatant advertising appeals. Purveyors of courses on how to get rich in real estate with nothing down, how to make a mint by going into business for yourself, and how to lose weight once and for all, know that it does not take much to find large numbers of people to buy into their appeals. We need to provide test questions in realistic, as well as obviously testlike, contexts. In particular, we need to understand and measure the "tacit knowledge" of everyday life (Wagner & Sternberg, 1985)—what people need to know to get along in a given environment that they are not explicitly taught.

The triarchic theory of intelligence is not the only contemporary theory of intelligence that might serve as a basis for expanding our notions of intelligence. Other such theories are Gardner's (1983) and Baron's (1985). The former theory, I believe, expands the domain of abilities measurement beyond those abilities that are truly "intelligence," whereas the later theory, in my opinion, unnecessarily restricts the range of intellectual abilities. But whatever theory one chooses to subscribe to, I believe that an advance of current theorizing is that it provides a basis for contemplating changes in tests that have remained essentially static for years, but that are now ready for a major change.

IMPLICATIONS FOR RESEARCH AND TESTING

The foregoing review suggests several directions for future research that I believe deserve priority in consideration of resource allocation. Topics are listed in terms of my own subjective ordering of priorities.

1. *Practical intelligence.* We seem to have reached a plateau in the predictive power of our current tests, especially as they pertain to predicting criteria that go beyond school grades. One possible reason for this plateau is

that intelligence in everyday life just doesn't seem to be the same thing as intelligence in academic settings. But most of a person's life is spent outside academe. Conceivably, some of the skills that lead to success in school settings may be maladaptive in other settings: Upper-level managers, for example, often complain that the best MBAs just don't have the knack for handling practical situations. We need to understand more about intelligence as it applies to everyday settings. What makes a smart manager or salesperson or detective? "Common sense" is often discussed but rarely researched. Perhaps the greatest breakthrough we could make in future research is to understand what common sense is and how it can be measured. Is it really a kind of "sense," or is it merely knowledge? Is it cross-situational, or fairly specific to given types of situations? The time has come to address and perhaps answer questions such as these.

2. *Creativity and nonentrenched thinking.* We are quite far along in terms of our ability to measure critical thinking but have hardly started in terms of our ability to measure creative or synthetic thinking. It is one thing to criticize ideas — another to come up with them. We need more research on how people come up with good ideas and how the ability to come up with such ideas can be measured. Of course, creativity tests have been around for years. But these tests, such as those of Torrance and Guilford, tend to trivialize the construct of creativity. How many unusual uses for a paper clip that a person can think of is not necessarily a good predictor of that person's ability to come up with meaningfully and significantly creative ideas. Thus, our need is for an understanding of consequential creativity and synthetic thinking, precisely the kind that is not measured by existing tests. Creativity is a difficult topic, and one that has attracted a greater quantity than quality of research. The time has come for more quality research on this topic.

3. *Executive processes in thinking.* Existing tests concentrate on the performance components of thinking. But more important than these components are the executive processes that choose, sequence, allocate, and evaluate these components. Research on metacognition got off to what I consider to have been a false start with an emphasis on what we know about our thinking rather than on how we control our thinking. Recent work has suggested that experts in a variety of domains often do not know much about how they solve problems: They are excellent metacognitively in the sense of executive control, but weak in the sense of understanding what they do. We need more research on executive control, rather than on knowledge of what we know.

4. *Automatization of information processing.* Experts are expert in a given field at least partly by virtue of their having automatized many aspects of performance that for nonexperts are controlled and conscious. For example, when I interact with graduate students, I am at an advantage vis-à-vis the students because many aspects of experimental design that are novel for them are automatic for me. As a result, I have more mental processing

resources than they do for dealing with the novelty inherent in a new project. Similarly, in driving, an experienced driver can be less susceptible to accidents because he or she has more mental resources left over to deal with novelty in road situations. We know relatively little about how information processing is automatized. There are essentially no practical tests of automatization. In order to understand and measure the development of intelligent expertise, such tests are needed.

5. *Talents.* The focus of test research and development has overwhelmingly been on conventionally defined aptitudes and achievements. Gardner (1983) has suggested that we need to expand our notions of intelligence to encompass talent domains such as the musical, kinesthetic, interpersonal, and so on. Although I would argue with Gardner as to whether the talent domains he considers all belong within the domain of intelligence, I think it is correct that understanding of the whole person requires going beyond traditional definitions of ability. Research on specialized talents is needed in order for us better to understand the cognitive and other bases for these propensities.

6. *Motivation.* Anyone who has worked with students at any level knows that a major element in student success is motivation to achieve. Since the early work on achievement motivation using projective tests, however, we have acquired relatively little understanding of how we might go about measuring motivation. Indeed, we have only the foggiest idea of what motivation is. Because of its importance to every kind of success, we need to understand better what motivation is and how it might be measured.

Efforts are now being made to broaden our bases for testing intellectual and other abilities. For example, I am currently developing a test—the Sternberg Triarchic Abilities Test—that will measure intelligence at the kindergarten through adult levels according to the precepts of the triarchic theory of intelligence. J.P. Das and Jack Naglieri are developing a test based upon Das's version of the theory of simultaneous and successive processing in cognition. Howard Gardner and David Feldman are developing a set of activities that departs substantially from multiple-choice format, again for the purpose of understanding abilities. Ann Brown and Joseph Campione have been devising instruments for measuring Vygotsky's construct of the zone of proximal development. All of these efforts have in common an underlying theoretical base for the development of tests of intelligence. In most cases, the underlying theories are complementary rather than mutually exclusive. I believe that the test development of the future will retain a closer link with cognitive theory than has ever been the case in the past. Such a link will provide a welcome response to the oft-made criticism that intelligence tests are atheoretical. The tests of the future will be better in part because they will be based on established theories of cognitive functioning.

Much of the current work on testing, including that sponsored by testing organizations such as ETS, is emphasizing the technology of testing. For example, ETS is sponsoring a major project on computerized testing. I think computers do hold great potential for improving testing, but not if they merely present on a computer screen what could be presented via a paper-and-pencil format. Moreover, adaptive testing is important because of the greater efficiency in testing that it yields, not because of the difference in what is measured. Hence, I believe that future funding should concentrate on new ideas, not on new technology, lest we end up measuring the same things we are now measuring, but in a fancier way. Testing will advance more by new ideas than by new technology. Ideally, the two will develop in unison. Such a pattern of development would maximize our future gains from ability tests of virtually all kinds.

REFERENCES

BARON, J. (1985). *Rationality and intelligence.* New York: Cambridge University Press.

CHI, M., GLASER, R., & REES, E. (1982). Expertise in problem solving. In R.J. Sternberg (Ed.), *Advances in the psychology of human intelligence* (Vol. 1). Hillsdale, NJ: Lawrence Erlbaum.

GARDNER, H. (1983). *Frames of mind: The theory of multiple intelligences.* New York: Basic Books.

HUNT, E. (1978). Mechanics of verbal ability. *Psychological Review, 85,* 109–130.

STERNBERG, R.J. (1977). *Intelligence, information processing, and analogical reasoning: The componential analysis of human abilities.* Hillsdale, NJ: Lawrence Erlbaum.

STERNBERG, R.J. (1985). *Beyond IQ: A triarchic theory of human intelligence.* New York: Cambridge University Press.

STERNBERG, R.J., & DAVIDSON, J.E. (1983). Insight in the gifted. *Educational Psychologist, 18,* 51–57.

STERNBERG, R.J., & POWELL, J.S. (1983). Comprehending verbal comprehension. *American Psychologist, 38,* 878–893.

WAGNER, R.K., & STERNBERG, R.J. (1985). Practical intelligence in real-world pursuits: The role of tacit knowledge. *Journal of Personality and Social Psychology, 49,* 436–458.

FIVE

IMPLICATIONS OF COGNITIVE PSYCHOLOGY FOR TESTING: CONTRIBUTIONS FROM WORK IN LEARNING STRATEGIES

Claire E. Weinstein
Debra K. Meyer

In this chapter, Claire E. Weinstein and Debra K. Meyer discuss the importance of measuring the processes of learning as well as the products of learning. Based on Weinstein's research over the last decade on the measurement of learning strategies and metacognition, as well as the work of other researchers, they discuss the advantages of moving from the measurement of knowledge to the measurement of learning. The measurement of learning includes the measurement of synthetic thinking, applications of learning, and acquisition of learning processes, as well as the measurement of learning strategies and metacognition. They find that improved student planning and self-control, improvements in classroom instruction, and classroom teaching follow from the measurement and use by teachers of test information about student learning strategies and metacognition.

INTRODUCTION

The last decade has witnessed a surge of interest in learning-to-learn phenomena from a wide variety of psychological perspectives (Anderson, 1985; Brown, Bransford, Ferrara, & Campione, 1983; Dillon & Schmeck, 1983; Kirby, 1984; Nickerson, Perkins, & Smith, 1985; Pressley & Levin, 1983a, 1983b; McCombs, 1988, Pintrich 1989; Schmeck, 1988; Weinstein & Mayer, 1986; Weinstein, Goetz, & Alexander, 1988; Wittrock, 1986; Zimmerman & Schunk, 1989). The data obtained by researchers in this area suggest that the effects of both student-directed learning and teacher-directed instructional activities depend partly on: what a learner *knows*, such as a student's prior knowledge about a topic or a related area; what a learner *thinks* about before, during, and after a learning activity, such as the types of strategic planning activities used; and what type of personal *context* the learner *generates* for a learning activity, such as the learner's motivational level or affective state. For the purposes of this chapter, attention will be focused on the subarea of learning-to-learn phenomena called learning strategies.

Studying and learning strategies include a variety of cognitive processes and behavioral skills designed to enhance learning effectiveness and efficiency, as well as the development of expertise. They have several characteristics in common. First, studying and learning strategies are always goal-directed activities. Second, they are intentionally invoked, which implies at least some level of conscious thought as well as active selection. This also means they are available for conscious reflection and description. Third, studying and learning strategies are effortful; they require time and often involve using multiple steps. Finally, they are not universally applicable. One's goals, the context, and the task conditions all interact to determine appropriate strategies to use.

CATEGORIES OF LEARNING STRATEGIES

As yet there is no generally accepted organizational scheme for classifying learning strategies. This is partially a reflection of the youth of the field and partly a reflection of the evolving literature and conceptualizations emanating from cognitive and educational psychology. However, Weinstein and Mayer (1986) attempted to create a preliminary set of categories that reflects the current state of research and practice. Although it is anticipated that this scheme will evolve and change over time, it is presented here to give an overview of learning strategies as a basis for the following discussion. Each category consists of techniques and processes that can be used by learners to impact knowledge acquisition, integration, and later retrieval. The ultimate goal of these activities is to enhance learning outcomes and performance.

Rehearsal Strategies for Basic Learning Tasks

These strategies emphasize simple repetition. For instance, repeating, in correct serial order, the biological classification system or the names of the colors in the spectrum are examples of rehearsal strategies for basic learning tasks. Many different educational tasks require simple recall. This is particularly true at the lower educational levels and in introductory courses at the postsecondary level. One of the key differences between experts and novices in a number of different content domains appears to be the knowledge base that they possess (Chi, 1978; Chi, Glaser, & Rees, 1982; Lesgold, 1984; Means & Voss, 1985). While the organization and integration of this knowledge is most important for expert decision making and problem solving, the acquisition of the basic knowledge needed to create a more unified data base is often the first step in these activities. In fact, it may not be possible for highly intelligent students to engage in deeper forms of information processing until they acquire a knowledge base on which to act (Schmeck, 1983).

One source of evidence for the importance of domain knowledge for the acquisition of expertise comes from research studies examining the effects of prior knowledge on reading comprehension. Recht & Leslie (1988) examined the effects of prior knowledge of baseball and expertise in reading on the recall of text about a baseball game. A qualitative measure of recall, how well students' recall of factual information compared to that of experts (semiprofessional baseball players), as well as a quantitative measure, how much was recalled, was obtained. Analysis of this data indicated that students with greater prior knowledge about baseball recalled more and were more similar to the experts in their recall of the text, regardless of their reading ability. The authors concluded: "... knowledge of a content domain is a powerful determinant of the amount and quality of information being recalled" (p. 19).

Another source of evidence for the importance of prior knowledge comes from a number of the researchers in cognitive and educational psychology who focus their efforts on defining thinking skills and the mechanisms by which they develop. A subset of studies in this area focus on the degree to which specific domain knowledge, reflective awareness, and strategy use interact to build expertise in specific classroom applications (e.g., Champagne, Klopfer, & Anderson, 1980), as well as across content domains (e.g., Perkins & Salomon, 1989). These results suggest that domain knowledge is a necessary but insufficient condition for acquiring strategies (Alexander & Judy, 1988), and expertise (Ennis, 1989).

The new conceptions of expertise and how it develops indicate that rote learning may have a necessary place in early learning within a domain, but ultimately success will depend on much more than the accumulation of relatively isolated facts. There are important implications of these findings for student assessment because expertise, or mastery, is no longer simply defined in terms of a core of factual information. How that information is organized and the strategies used to create, maintain, integrate, and access it are at least equally important. Therefore, simple tests of knowledge are not adequate for examining the development or nature of expert performance.

We must also identify and evaluate students' awareness and knowledge about cognitive learning strategies and their use of these strategies. Thus, multiple criterion measures are needed to evaluate student learning and performance.

Rehearsal Strategies for Complex Learning Tasks

Tasks included in this category extend beyond the superficial learning of unrelated bits of information and simple lists. Common strategies in this category include underlining notes or a portion of text, and taking notes in a lecture class. Generally, these methods are designed to facilitate literal reproduction. (However, although note-taking behaviors may be classified as rehearsal in the case of a literal reproduction of a lecture which is common in the fast pace of traditional classrooms, they may be classified as elaboration if the note taker is transforming the lecture into a personally meaningful form, which is more common when taking notes from text or when reviewing notes, situations in which the note taker has control over the pacing.)

Like the methods described under basic rehearsal strategies, these complex rehearsal strategies seem particularly effective when they provide further opportunities for more meaningful processing to take place, such as the use of elaboration, organization, or comprehension monitoring. For example, Shrager & Mayer (1989) reported a study in which some students who were classified as having little knowledge of cameras were directed to take notes. These low-knowledge note takers were more successful on meaningful recall tasks than their low-knowledge non-note-taking peers, but were not more successful on verbatim recall. In addition, students who were rated high in camera knowledge did not benefit from note taking. Kiewra (1988) has suggested that note-taking research needs to begin to investigate the interactions among prior knowledge, control-processing abilities, and strategy use on both note taking and the review of notes. Here, too, the data support the suggestion that multiple criterion measures are needed to assess performance more sensitively. Looking at a single factor or process may result in missing other important contributing processes affecting the learning outcomes (Alexander & Judy, 1988; Garner, 1987; Kiewra, 1988).

Elaboration Strategies for Basic Learning Tasks

Elaboration can be accomplished in a variety of ways, such as using mental imagery to describe an event in history or relating the capitals of each state to the state name by creating a sentence. In each of these cases elaboration involves adding some sort of symbolic construction to what one is trying to learn to make it more meaningful. For example, Pressley, Symons, McDaniel, Snyder, & Turnure (1988) found that subjects who justified their elaborations and subjects who formed mental images of relationships among difficult, seemingly unrelated, factual material were more successful on recall tasks than those who did not elaborate.

Like rehearsal strategies, elaboration strategies for basic learning tasks also help to generate the knowledge base needed for the development of expertise. However, in addition, the use of elaboration strategies often facilitates the integration of our world knowledge by generating relationships among information in our knowledge base (Wittrock, 1990).

Elaboration Strategies for Complex Learning Tasks

The major goal of strategies in this category also requires getting learners involved in building bridges between what they already know, have experience in or believe, and what they are trying to understand. Methods in this category include summarizing, paraphrasing, creating analogies, and using prior knowledge, experience, attitudes, and beliefs to help make the new information more meaningful. Trying to apply a principle to everyday experience, relating what was presented in a textbook to a class discussion, paraphrasing an argument, relating the events in a play to a family outing, all of these are different ways to elaborate.

Elaboration strategies for complex tasks have been shown to be effective in a variety of classroom settings, across ages and ability levels. For example, Alexander, White, Haensly, & Crimmins-Jeanes (1987) trained average fourth graders, gifted eighth graders, and average tenth graders in general analogical reasoning skills which were later reinforced in instruction from their regular classroom teachers. These researchers found that analogy training proved to be beneficial for students in all grades and across all levels of ability based on a posttest comparison with a control group, and scores on a near-transfer task. In addition, the benefits of the analogical training were still evident six weeks later on a delayed posttest. Swing and Peterson (1988) reported that adjunct questions that asked fifth-grade students to elaborate and integrate the concepts being practiced on math worksheets improved recall on tests measuring the concepts, particularly for high-ability students. Swing, Stoiber, and Peterson (1988) focused on instructing students to use the cognitive strategies of defining, describing, comparing and justifying, and summarizing in problem-solving tasks. This research demonstrated the effectiveness of such training by regular classroom teachers especially for students in low-ability classrooms. Furthermore, Swing et al. demonstrated that individual student ability and class ability are separate but important considerations for the teaching of learning strategies and skills. The experimental program was found to be most effective for medium- to high-ability classrooms and, individually, for low-ability students.

Organization Strategies for Basic Learning Tasks

Organization strategies are used to transform information into another format that is easier to understand. The benefits of using organization strategies appear to be due to both the processing involved in accomplishing the transformation and the structure imposed. Listing foreign words by their part of speech, grouping paintings by the artist, and using a time line to list events are all examples of organization strategies. In each of these examples an existing or created scheme is used to impose organization on an otherwise unordered set of items. It is also important to note that organization strategies, like elaboration strategies, require a more active role on the part of the learner than do simple rote or rehearsal strategies.

An example of research in this area is the study by Muir, Masterson, Wiener, Lyon, and White (1989) comparing the effects of training gifted and above-average students in the organization strategy of categorization on their recall of word lists. The subjects were elementary and junior high school students who were assessed in terms of their (1) strategic functioning (use of the categorization strategy), (2) knowledge base (as measured by I.Q.), (3) generalization to transfer tasks, and (4) speed of processing. The use of the organization strategy was the best predictor of recall for the above-average students whereas speed of processing was the best predictor for the gifted students.

Organization Strategies for Complex Learning Tasks

Examples from this category include outlining chapters from a text, creating a conceptual map, and creating a hierarchy of sources to use in writing a term paper. Here, too, it is both the process and the product that seem to contribute to the effectiveness of the method.

The development of expertise in radiology is a good example of how learning strategies can be used to organize and access knowledge. Lesgold (1984) discussed expertise in radiology as being characterized by schema development and refinement. Schema, in this context, are organized clusters of knowledge represented as a set of assumptions or rules for interpreting new information. Expert radiologists were found to possess more detailed schema for diagnosis than interns. In addition, the experts based their more accurate and faster diagnosis on fewer aspects of an x-ray. The organization of a diagnosis around a group of symptoms is part of what is considered expertise in this area and serves to exemplify the usefulness of organizing knowledge.

Comprehension Monitoring Strategies

The term metacognition refers to individuals' knowledge about their own cognitive processes as well as to their abilities to control these processes by organizing, implementing, monitoring, and modifying them as a function of learning outcomes and feedback. A subarea within metacognition that is particularly relevant to the present discussion is called comprehension monitoring. Operationally, comprehension monitoring involves establishing learning goals, assessing the degree to which these goals are being met, and, if necessary, modifying the strategies being used to facilitate goal attainment. For example, using self-questioning to check understanding of material presented in class and attempting to apply a new principle are both ways to assess one's level of understanding.

A major difference between experts and novices is that experts have well-developed self-monitoring skills (Chi & Glaser, 1988), whereas novices do not have the background to monitor as effectively. The progression of strategy choices evidenced by elementary students learning the concept of volume was reported by Burbles and Linn (1988). These authors found a variation among students in their individual tolerances for anomalies. Some students changed their thinking without any feedback, while some changed upon being presented with a contradiction, and still others did not change until a written rule was given. Novices' awareness and beliefs about which variables were important appeared to influence the monitoring of their learning and their acquisition of the knowledge.

Detection of inconsistencies in reading is another example of a metacognitive behavior. Prior knowledge, skill in reading, and metacognitive awareness are a few of the variables that have been found to affect students' comprehension monitoring in reading. Vosniadou, Pearson, and Rogers (1988) found that familiarity with domain knowledge can affect whether or not inconsistencies are detected in text. These authors studied the effects of prior knowledge of the context of the story and familiarity with the story on how inconsistencies were represented and compared. Familiarity with the content appeared to be the key variable in successfully detecting inconsistencies. Cross and Paris (1988) reported that assessing students' awareness of person, task, and strategy variables, as well as their awareness of their level of performance, may be critical to designing appropriate interventions. Reading awareness was measured in two interviews: (1) one interview asked students to evaluate the task difficulty and their own ability, as well as their plans for goal attainment and monitoring of progress toward a goal; and (2) a second interview asked students to rate the usefulness of particular strategies. Reading performance was assessed by a series of tasks from a classroom reading inventory. Students were pre- and posttested with experimental groups receiving the Informed Strategies for Learning program during the school year (Paris, Cross, & Lipson, 1984). Older (ten-year-old) children's reading awareness and reading performance were more similar than those of younger (eight-year-old) children. Third graders who were low on both awareness and performance measures did not benefit from an intervention program, however, those low in performance but having some awareness did benefit. These findings indicated that some minimum level of awareness may be needed before successfully instructing students in metacognitive skills, or that different instructional methods are necessary for individuals whose levels of awareness are minimal. Again, the need for assessment methods that are broader in scope than simple achievement tests or simple recall of prior knowledge is highlighted.

Affective Strategies

Affective support strategies help to create and maintain suitable internal climates for learning. They help to generate a context in which effective studying and learning can take place, and they seem to be influenced by such variables as the content domain and task demands. Many affective strategies are designed to impact students' motivation or attitude toward studying and learning, as well as the degree to which they value the outcomes of these activities.

Students' general attitudes toward studying and learning, as well as their motivation for succeeding, have a great impact on their diligence, particularly in autonomous situations in which much of the work must be done on their own, such as completing assignments outside of class. If one cannot generate some interest in the task (even if this interest is simply to get it over with!) then it will be very difficult to put forth the appropriate effort to complete it, particularly if the task is a difficult one. Knowing which learning strategies to use to accomplish a study or learning objective is not sufficient—one must also want to use them. This valuing component is critical to action. Many students and trainees know a lot more about how to study and learn than they actually use. The translation of our various types of knowledge about how to study and learn into actual strategies that are implemented in an effective manner is mediated primarily by support strategies in the context of our own goals and our beliefs about our chances of succeeding. Ames and Archer (1988) found that gifted junior high school students' perceived competence and perception of the classroom goal orientation (mastery versus performance) were predictive of the students' reported use of learning strategies. Students in mastery-oriented learning environments were found to report using more study and learning strategies. This research suggests that a variable contributing to students' use or lack of use of learning strategies may be their perception of their classrooms' goal orientation.

The effects of motivational factors on the acquisition of knowledge, as well as the development and use of strategies, is an evolving, much-needed area of research (Alexander & Judy, 1988). Paris and his colleagues have repeatedly concluded that cognitive skill is fully realized only when it is matched with motivational will (Paris, Cross, & Lipson, 1984; Paris, Lipson, & Wixson, 1983). Posner (1988) discussed the need for including motivational variables in studies examining the development of expertise. Pintrich (1989) discussed the results of two studies of the relationships between motivation and self-regulation among high school and college students. The results of the path analyses suggest that when students report using self-regulation they are more likely to report higher levels of self-efficacy. Both self-regulation and self-efficacy were found to be influenced positively when students intrinsically valued the learning of the content and negatively when students reported higher levels of test anxiety. The data suggested that cognitive skills may be more important than self-perceptions in terms of classroom achievement and emphasized the need to understand better how self-efficacy and self-regulation interact to produce varying performance outcomes.

THE ASSESSMENT OF LEARNING STRATEGIES

The issue of how to assess appropriately an individual's capacity to benefit from instruction and study has increased rapidly in importance in educational research. There are two major reasons for this increased interest in methods of assessment: (1) the pressing need to prepare educationally disadvantaged students for the rigors of higher education, and (2) the growth of cognitive information-processing theories and research in applied settings. The development of learning strategies training programs and the increased interest in applied cognitive psychology have highlighted several problems related to the area of assessment. Most notably, the difficulty with assessing individuals' strengths and weaknesses in strategy knowledge and use has emerged. Confounding this problem of diagnosis is a problem common to many fields of study and that is the lack of basic definitions which are shared by researchers and developers of learning strategies assessment instruments and programs of instruction.

Implications for Assessment from Work with Underprepared Students

Large numbers of academically underprepared or disadvantaged students are entering postsecondary institutions. In response to this influx of students with special needs, many institutions have created special programs to address academic deficits (Noel & Levitz, 1982; Weinstein & Underwood, 1985). However, the successful implementation and evaluation of training programs and courses designed to teach learning strategies requires reliable and valid means for measuring students' entry-level deficits and their progress. Having the means to diagnose student deficits could contribute significantly to the design of instruction and having the means to monitor progress and course outcomes could contribute significantly to evaluating and improving the effectiveness of the training.

Unfortunately, the majority of the instruments currently available in either a published or an experimental form, were developed during the 1960s and focus primarily on student study practices (e.g., Brown, 1964; Brown & Holtzman, 1967; Christensen, 1968). These measures are generally used in high school or postsecondary educational and training settings to predict future academic performance, counsel students about their study methods, or screen students for entry into developmental study skills courses. Whereas all these inventories predict grade-point average from a low to a moderate degree (0.19 to 0.60), they do not produce specific information that could be used to facilitate individual student remediation. They tend to focus on what Svensson (1977) calls a correlational approach: they provide information about the conditions under which an individual studies best but not the methods and cognitive processes they use to do it.

This focus on correlates of effective studying, rather than variables directly related to success in school, limits the usefulness of these measures for formulating remediation plans for individuals or groups of students. Because remediation of student deficits is a major goal of much of the applied work in cognitive psychology, it appears that a change in focus is needed in the methods used to assess student studying and learning strategies.

Implications for Assessment
from Current Cognitive Research

The second major reason for the increasing interest in the area of assessment relates to both basic and applied research in information processing. Paralleling the need to refocus how learning and studying strategies are assessed is the viewpoint in cognitive and educational psychology that attention needs to be directed at the processes of learning rather than at its products. The measurement issue in cognitive research is a major stumbling block to progress (see Garner, 1987, 1988, for a discussion of this issue). Because cognitive researchers focus on topics that reflect processes that are usually not available to direct measurement, indirect forms of assessment must be developed for more precise research hypotheses to be amenable to study. In response to this need there has been a renewed focus on variations of self-report methodologies that could be used to help gather data about covert strategies (e.g., Pintrich et al., 1988; Weinstein & Palmer, 1990; Weinstein, Schulte & Palmer, 1987).

In addition to the difficulty in measuring cognitive processing which cannot be directly observed, the lack of a consistent definition of studying and learning strategies across existing instruments presents a more immediate hurdle for assessment. Even the term study skills is used to refer to a broad range of topics. Furthermore, inventories vary in their coverage of these topics and the specific topics included in a particular inventory often are not specified. This makes it very difficult to compare the author's and the user's conceptions of what is being measured and how it can be used.

THE LEARNING AND STUDY STRATEGIES INVENTORY

In an attempt to address many of the shortcomings of previous instruments, Weinstein, Schulte, and Palmer (1987) developed the *Learning and Study*

Strategies Inventory (LASSI). The LASSI is designed to measure college students' use of learning and studying strategies and methods. (A parallel instrument, the Learning and Study Strategies Inventory–High School version [LASSI–HS] has also been developed for use with ninth, tenth, eleventh, and twelfth grades [Weinstein and Palmer, 1990].) The LASSI is a diagnostic and prescriptive measure that focuses on both covert and overt thoughts and behaviors that relate to successful learning and that can be altered through educational interventions.

The LASSI is designed to be used as: (1) a diagnostic measure to help identify areas in which students could benefit most from educational interventions; (2) a basis for planning individual prescriptions for both remediation and enrichment; (3) a pre-post achievement measure for students participating in programs or courses focusing on study skills and learning strategies; (4) an evaluation tool to assess the degree of success of intervention courses or programs; and (5) a counseling tool for college orientation programs, developmental education programs, learning assistance programs, and learning centers. Currently, the LASSI is being used for one or more of these purposes in over 750 colleges and universities in the United States and in more than 18 foreign countries.

Administration and Scoring of the LASSI

The *Learning and Study Strategies Inventory* is a 77-item self-report instrument. The LASSI includes the following ten scales: Attitude, Motivation, Time Management, Anxiety, Concentration, Information Processing, Selecting Main Ideas, Study Aids, Self Testing, and Test Strategies. The individual items on each scale are written in a Likert format. The students respond to these items by reporting the degree to which each one represents their own attitudes, thoughts, or behaviors. (Examples of items from each scale are presented in the next section). A total score for the instrument is not computed. Instead, ten individual scale scores are derived. These ten scores can be compared to national norms or to percentile cutoff scores. No total score is calculated because the purpose of the LASSI is to diagnose in which of the ten areas, if any, a student may need remedial assistance or enrichment. The scale scores for the LASSI have demonstrated a high degree of stability with coefficient alphas for the scales in the range of 0.68 to 0.86, and test-retest correlation coefficients ranging from 0.72 to 0.85.

The LASSI Scales

The development of the LASSI was the result of an extensive review of existing and experimental study skills materials and programs, the judgment of experts in the evolving field of teaching students strategies for learning, a series of interviews and questionnaire studies with students in postsecondary educational settings, and psychometric studies using prototype instruments.

Frameworks for organizing learning and study strategies like that of Weinstein and Mayer (1986) were not yet available. Nevertheless, the scales do reflect the categories of learning strategies outlined previously: rehearsal strategies, elaboration strategies, organizational strategies, comprehension monitoring strategies, and affective strategies. In addition, the scales assess strategies that are external to the learner, the content, or the task. These strategies help the learner control the learning environment as well as the processing of the new information. For example, participation in study groups, the use of study guides, or the use of adjunct questions presented in text are strategies that are available to students for their implementation.

Three of the scales address the general category of affective strategies. General attitudes toward school have a great impact on how hard students will work, particularly when studying alone. The Attitude Scale includes items that measure students' interests and goals in college. How important is college to them? How does attending college and finishing a degree fit with what they want out of life? How clear are they about their educational goals? A sample item is: "I feel confused and undecided as to what my educational goals should be." If school does not fit well with students' personal goals, then it is less likely that they will be interested or willing to work at succeeding. Students' diligence, self-discipline, and willingness to work hard as it relates to specific academic tasks are reflected in the degree of responsibility they demonstrate for achieving academic goals. Such variables are examined in the Motivation Scale. "I set high standards for myself in school" is an example of an item on this scale. However, regardless of the degree to which they value their education and the commitment they make to taking responsibility for their learning, many students' performance is compromised due to their high level of anxiety. On the Anxiety Scale the degree to which students' self-doubts and perceptions of stress interfere with their academic performance is addressed. To what degree do students direct their attention away from the task at hand because of anxious thinking? A typical item from this scale would be: "Worrying about doing poorly interfered with my concentration on tests."

In addition to internal support strategies for maintaining a positive attitude, high motivation, and an optimal level of anxiety, students can also impact their performance in educational settings by manipulating the learning environment, the allocation of learning resources, their use of learning aids, and their use of cognitive learning strategies. Time management practices, such as organization and scheduling of school work, are assessed on the Time Management Scale with items like: "When I decide to study I set aside a specific length of time and I stick with it." Another important part of effective and efficient learning is reflected in the students' ability to make time to learn while dealing with competing goals, distractions, and procrastination. The degree to which a student can concentrate and stay focused in the face of both internal and external distractions is assessed on the Concentration Scale. For example, an item assessing concentration is: "I find that during lectures I think of other things and don't really listen to what is being said." Knowing how to use information organized by others (e.g., textbooks, study guides, etc.), as well as how to adapt or create study aids for personal use, is another set of methods students need to know in order to improve the effectiveness and efficiency of their learning. Students' use of organizational aids, techniques, materials, or assistance which help them to understand and remember new information is assessed in the Study Aids Scale. A typical item from this scale would be: "When they are available, I attend group review sessions." Common types of rehearsal strategies such as those involved in note taking during lectures, or highlighting notes or text material, are also measured on the Study Aids Scale.

The LASSI scales also assesses students' use of elaboration and organization strategies. "I translate what I am studying into my own words" is a sample item from the Information Processing Scale. This scale measures several subareas including the use of mental imagery, verbal elaboration, comprehension monitoring, and reasoning. Students need a wide variety of methods to help them make new information more meaningful. Such methods can be as simple as learning to paraphrase course material in their own words or as complex as methods involving reasoning skills. Along with relating new knowledge to prior knowledge, students must also identify what parts of the new information are important for further study. The degree to which students can focus on the key points, whether reading a textbook or listening to a lecture, is examined in the Selecting Main Ideas Scale with items such as: "I have difficulty identifying the important points in my reading."

Our present system of education requires that student learning be demonstrated through formal assessments and examinations. The methods students use to prepare for and take tests are addressed in the Test Strategies Scale of the LASSI. How students prepare to take a test and the methods they use while taking a test are measured with items such as: "I find I have misunderstood what is wanted and lose points because of it." Finally, the students' ongoing ability to review and assess their own understanding is measured on the Self Testing Scale. Most of the items on this scale measure some aspect of comprehension monitoring. This scale examines how students review materials and prepare for classes and exams. Without the continual review and testing of knowledge, learning would be incomplete, and errors or misconceptions could go undetected. For example, a sample item from the Self Testing Scale is: "I stop periodically while reading and mentally go over or review what was said."

IMPLICATIONS FOR RESEARCH AND ASSESSMENT OF LEARNING STRATEGIES

In a very short time the area of learning strategies has made phenomenal progress and has been applied to a variety of educational and training settings. The attention given to research and development in this area reflects the compelling questions which are generated when researchers and practitioners attempt to account for variations in learning given different types of individuals, different learning environments, a variety of methods for acquiring knowledge, and an array of content domains. The interaction among these variables is as complex as it is intriguing, and our quest for understanding these relationships generates five possible areas for further study:

1. Refining our understanding of the cognitive processes underlying studying and learning and how they can best be assessed,
2. Understanding how learning strategies develop from their initial acquisition through integration and automatization,
3. Understanding how individuals' knowledge of learning strategies interacts with various content domains,
4. Systematically investigating how learning strategies and knowledge are transferred to content domains different from the ones in which they were acquired, and
5. Investigating methods that can evaluate individuals' metacognitive processes and use of control.

These five interrelated areas of research are not a comprehensive list of "things to do" in studying learning-to-learn, nor are they new questions. However, focusing on this set of questions helps to suggest some important considerations for researchers and developers of instruments to assess studying and learning.

1. Refining our understanding of the cognitive processes underlying studying and learning and how they can best be assessed. What are the cognitive processes underlying effective studying and learning? How can they best be measured? Current achievement tests do not address students' awareness about or use of learning strategies. Garner and Alexander (1989) expanded on this observation and suggested that perhaps the ways in which we measure the effects of strategy instruction also need to be reexamined. With respect to the finding that general measures of achievement do not appear to be affected by strategy instruction, Garner and Alexander propose that we review two questions: (1) How much time is needed to become proficient in the use of a strategy? and (2) Can strategies be taught in a way that enhances students' performance on general tests of achievement? These questions address issues about transfer of strategy knowledge as well as when strategies are used, but they also address the issue of how we identify strategy use. Moreover, the complex nature of learning becomes apparent when we attempt to measure an ongoing process with its products. We can use a "dip stick" method of checking learning along the way or, when it is appropriate, use a final measure of achievement. The degree to which they are robust, generalizable, and transferable will be equally, if not more important for future learning

2. Understanding how learning strategies develop from their initial acquisition through integration and automatization. How are new strategies acquired, integrated, and automatized? By comparing novices and experts, researchers have indirectly attempted to answer this question. Within and across domains there appear to be common characteristics of both novices and experts. As discussed previously, Lesgold (1984) found novices in radiology to use a more generalized schema in diagnosis, requiring more symptoms in order to verify a disease. The experienced radiologists, on the other hand, appeared to utilize more refined schema and thus looked for the presence of a few revealing symptoms that made diagnosis more accurate. Ericsson and Polson (1988) reported that an expert headwaiter encoded orders by categorizing the items, whereas inexperienced waiters attempted to remember orders sequentially.

Research has also indicated that novices are lacking in both the amount and the quality of their knowledge structures (e.g., Chi, Glaser, & Rees, 1982). In a developmental study of expertise, Means and Voss (1985) found differences in representation to be mainly quantitative. The major advantage for older experts was simply more prior knowledge. Thus, amount of knowledge is an important consideration.

In addition to smaller knowledge structures, novices also appear to have poorer access to and utilization of their knowledge. Another related qualitative difference associated with expert-like performance is more cohesive and integrated knowledge bases (Gobbo & Chi, 1986). Cohesion has been demonstrated by expert physicists in their selection and application of physics principles in a single step (Larkin, McDermott, Simon, & Simon, 1980). Novice physics students have been found to draw general laws from prototypes rather than from principles, as their instructors would (Green, McCloskey, & Carramazza, 1985). Knowledge representation and accessibility of knowledge are intertwined, and the ways in which novices access knowledge are interesting novice-expert distinctions. The accessing of knowledge can be observed indirectly by identifying the strategies subjects use when solving a problem. Larkin et al. (1985) found that novices in physics moved from the statement of the problem to its mathematical representation, and spent most of their "think" time deciding which mathematical equation was appropriate for the solution. On the other hand, experts spent the most time deciding on the underlying physics principle in the problem and then moved quickly to selecting the applicable mathematical expression.

What are characteristics and learning activities that enable some novices to move along the continuum toward expertise? What factors distinguish between successful learners and unsuccessful learners in terms of prior knowledge, strategy use, and procedural knowledge? Increasingly, researchers in cognitive, developmental, and educational psychology have begun to assess individual differences that help in determining which novices acquire expertise. These issues probe individual differences among novices, such as prior knowledge and experience, as well as individual goal orientations, personal beliefs, tolerance for incongruity, and many other affective variables.

Siegler and Jenkins (1989) discussed the discovery and subsequent acquisition of a math strategy in five-year-old children. One of the major points the authors made is that strategies compete, and the choice of using one strategy over others depends on whether the goal is efficiency or accuracy. In addition, it appears that personal preferences for strategies, or strong associations between a strategy and the context (including content-domain and task characteristics) are some other possible explanations for strategy selection and use. Among the many other questions these authors raise about modeling strategy acquisition based on their research are: Under what conditions is a particular strategy utilized, and how aware of a strategy does a learner need to be in order to optimally benefit from its implementation?

Currently no instruments exist that assess the level of development of students learning strategy repertoires or even their understanding and use of a particular strategy. In addition, we need to learn more about the potential roles of awareness and control variables in strategy acquisition and use and about how these variables can be measured.

3. *Understanding how individuals' knowledge of learning strategies interacts with various content domains.* What is included in an individual's repertoire of learning strategies? How do these strategies interact with domain knowledge? An area that is related to the issues of acquiring and appropriately transferring cognitive learning strategies is the role of general and domain knowledge in learning and thinking (Alexander & Judy, 1988; Brown, Collins, & Duguid, 1989; Ennis, 1989; Garner & Alexander, 1989; Perkins & Salomon, 1989; Perkins & Simmons, 1988). After a review of the literature in the areas of domain knowledge and strategic knowledge, Alexander and Judy (1988) emphasized the need to look at the interaction between these two types of knowledge acquisition. Furthermore, Alexander and Judy highlighted research that indicated that affective variables, such as the type or level of motivation, may alter how content domains and cognitive processing strategies are acquired and used. Garner and Alexander (1989) suggested that understanding the interaction between domain knowledge and strategy use is crucial for better understanding metacognitive processes. They hypothesized that a certain amount of content knowledge may be necessary before strategy instruction is effective.

As mentioned previously, current findings in cognitive and educational psychology emphasize a shift from a content-is-sufficient-for-expertise to a content-is-necessary-for-expertise position (Alexander & Judy, 1988; Perkins & Salomon, 1989; Pressley, Symons, McDaniel, Snyder, & Turnure, 1988). There also appears to be a return to considering the role of general strategy use in addition to domain-specific strategies. Recently developed expert systems exemplify the importance of general heuristics in expertise (e.g.

Larkin, Reif, Carbonell, & Gugliotta, 1988; Kulkarni & Simon, 1988). Voss, Blais, Means, Greene, and Ahwesh (1986) found that instruction in economics did not necessarily lead to better performance in solving day-to-day economics problems. However, a college education was found to be related to greater metacognitive awareness and reasoning. Research has not yet been able to untangle how the general problem-solving skills of experts are tied into their in-depth knowledge of the content. Because a major goal of education is to provide a knowledge base that will transfer to the next level of instruction or the work place, understanding better how general and domain-specific knowledge interact is central to preparing individuals for the future.

4. Systematically investigating how learning strategies and knowledge are transferred to content domains different from the ones in which they were acquired. How are learning strategies and knowledge transferred to new situations? The issues of continued use and transfer are critical for both theory development and application in the area of learning to learn. Many models of human functioning are predicted on at least a degree of self-regulation of cognitive processes and behavior (Zimmerman & Schunk, 1989). Why bother to teach learning strategies or remediate student deficits if the strategies and skills acquired will largely be abandoned after the training? A major difference between experts and novices lies in the strategic nature of their approach to various learning, problem-solving, decision-making, and reasoning tasks (Larkin, 1985). How can we foster the development of expertise if learners often do not appropriately use and transfer the strategies they are taught? This is a particularly thorny question for our society since many educationally disadvantaged and minority students are not prepared to take advantage of advanced educational opportunities and training. Providing simple remediation based on a model of delivering only declarative and procedural information about learning strategies does not appear to be sufficient.

Without a better understanding of transfer, how can our assessments of learning be valid representations of the knowledge we believe the student is demonstrating? Salomon and Perkins (1989) cautioned that part of the problem with any discussion of transfer is the definitions and perspectives each individual investigator, or developer of instructional materials and assessments brings to it. For example, Salomon and Perkins noted that we need to distinguish between transfer and learning, between what is transferred and how it is transferred, and between how much is transferred and how far from the original content and context of acquisition the knowledge is transferred. They suggest two mechanisms of transfer that take into account some of these issues. Low-Road mechanisms of transfer deal with knowledge that is highly automatized and evoked with little reflective thinking. For example, sitting down at a computer terminal as opposed to a typewriter often evokes a transfer of our typing skills with only minor adjustments for differences in types or functions of keys. On the other hand, Salomon and Perkins proposed

High-Road transfer as the explicit abstraction of knowledge and its use in a context different from the one in which it was acquired. Thus, researchers and developers of assessment instruments need to consider and be explicit about what aspects of knowledge they are measuring. Is it really transfer of knowledge or learning?

5. *Investigating methods that can evaluate individuals' metacognitive processes and use of control.* How do you evaluate an individual's metacognitive processes and use of executive control (Garner, 1987, 1988)? Why do learners often abandon their strategies? Part of the answer appears to lie in the interaction of conditional knowledge (which focuses on when it is and is not appropriate to use a particular strategy), control processes, and affective variables with the acquisition of strategies for learning content knowledge and developing expertise in an area (Paris, Lipson, & Wixson, 1983; Baker, Armbruster, & Baker, 1986; Zimmerman & Schunk, 1989). As part of conditional knowledge a rationale is provided for using the strategy. This rationale includes relating the strategy to the learner's goal, the task requirements, the context, and the resources available to the learner. All these steps are designed to give the learner more control over the task and how it is accomplished. Control processes are used to help the learner plan, implement, monitor, and modify, if necessary, a cognitive course of action. The major affective variables that appear to impact strategy use include the learner's goals and goal orientation (e.g., intrinsic versus extrinsic), the task value (e.g., interest level, importance, and utility value), expectancies (e.g., Can I do the task? Will I succeed?), anxiety, and emotional reactions (e.g., pride and fear) (Locke, Shaw, Saari, & Latham, 1981; McCombs, 1989; Pintrich, 1988, 1989; Zimmerman & Schunk, 1989).

One of the difficulties in assessing whether individuals are monitoring and modifying their thinking was demonstrated by Hunter-Blanks, Ghatala, Pressley, and Levin (1988). When subjects were given sentences varying in the difficulty of remembering them, the subjects indicated that they were ready to be tested on the sentences prematurely, although they had noted the more difficult sentences and had spent more time studying them. Only after they were tested on the sentences were they able to accurately predict the differential difficulty in recalling the sentences. Hunter-Blanks et al. concluded that errors are not necessarily indicators of whether monitoring has occurred, and asking subjects about readiness to be tested is not the same as asking them how difficult the material was to study. Thus, the questions we think we are asking, whether in a research paradigm or on a self-report inventory, may not be the same questions the subjects, students, or examinees think they are answering.

In their recent review of metacognitive research, Garner and Alexander (1989) discussed what we know about metacognition and proposed an agenda for future research. From their review of the literature they draw three general conclusions: (1) metacognition develops with age and experience,

(2) failures in comprehension monitoring are frequent regardless of age or skill, and (3) some strategies are difficult to learn and, as noted previously, some strategies are easy to abandon. The Garner and Alexander suggested the use of multiple-method assessment to provide converging evidence as one of the ways in which we can further our understanding of metacognitive processes. This methodological approach proved valuable to Swing, Stoiber, and Peterson (1988) and is essential to avoiding the problem mentioned above: that our questions may not be interpreted in the ways in which we intended or our observations alone may not be valid. Findings like these strongly suggest that asking about or measuring one aspect of an individual's studying and learning strategies is inadequate for diagnosing strengths and weaknesses, or for suggesting methods to provide remediation or enrichment.

REFERENCES

ALEXANDER, P.A., & JUDY, J.E. (1988). The interaction of domain-specific and strategic knowledge in academic performance. *Review of Educational Research, 58*(4), 375–404.

ALEXANDER, P.A., WHITE, C.S., HAENSLY, P.A., CRIMMINS-JEANES, M. (1987). Training in analogical reasoning. *American Education Research Journal, 24*(3), 387–404.

AMES, C., & ARCHER, J. (1988). Achievement goals in the classroom: Students' learning strategies and motivational processes. *Journal of Educational Psychology, 80*(3), 260–267.

ANDERSON, J.R. (1985). *Cognitive psychology and its implications.* San Francisco: Freeman.

BAKER, A.L., ARMBRUSTER, B.B., & BAKER, L. (1986). The role of metacognition in reading and studying. In J. Orasanu (Ed.), *Reading comprehension from research to practice* (pp. 49–75). Hillsdale, NJ: Lawrence Erlbaum.

BROWN, A.L., BRANSFORD, J.F., FERRARA, R., & CAMPIONE, J. (1983). Learning, remembering, and understanding. In J. Flavell & E. Markman (Eds.), *Handbook of child psychology* (Vol. 3, pp. 77–166). New York: Wiley.

BROWN, J.S., COLLINS, A., & DUGUID, P. (1989). Situated cognition and the culture of learning. *Educational Researcher 18*(1), 32–42.

BROWN, W.F. (1964). *Effective study test.* San Marcos, TX: Effective Study Materials.

BROWN, W.F., & HOLTZMAN, W.H. (1967). *Survey of study habits and attitudes.* New York: The Psychological Corporation.

BURBLES, N.C., & LINN, M.C. (1988). Response to contradiction: Scientific reasoning during adolescence. *Journal of Educational Psychology, 80*(1), 67–75.

CHAMPAGNE, A.B., KLOPFER, L.E., & ANDERSON, J.H. (1980). Factors influencing the learning of classical mechanics. *American Journal of Physics, 48*(12) 1074–1079.

CHI, M.T.H. (1978). Knowledge structure and memory development. In R. Siegler (Ed.), *Children's thinking: What develops?* (pp. 73–96). Hillsdale, NJ: Lawrence Erlbaum.

CHI, M.T.H., & GLASER, R. (1988). Overview. In M.T.H. Chi, R. Glaser, & M.J. Farr (Eds.), *The nature of expertise* (pp. 15–27). Hillsdale, NJ: Lawrence Erlbaum.

CHI, M.T.H., GLASER, R., & REES, E. (1982). Expertise in problem solving. In R. Sternberg (Ed.), *Advances in the psychology of human intelligence* (Vol. 1, pp. 1–115). Hillsdale, NJ: Lawrence Erlbaum.

CHRISTENSEN, F.A. (1968). *College adjustment and study skills inventory.* Berea, OH: Personal Growth Press.

CROSS, D.R., & PARIS, S.G. (1988). Developmental and instructional analyses of children's metacognition and reading comprehension. *Journal of Educational Psychology, 80*(2), 131–142.

DILLON, R.F., & SCHMECK, R.R. (1983). *Individual differences in cognition.* New York: Academic Press.

ENNIS, R.H. (1989). Critical thinking and subject specificity: Clarification and needed research. *Educational Researcher* 18(3), 4–10.

ERICSSON, K.A., & POLSON, P.G. (1988). A cognitive analysis of exceptional memory for restaurant orders. In M.T.H. Chi, R. Glaser, & M.J. Farr (Eds.), *The nature of expertise* (pp. 23–70). Hillsdale, NJ: Lawrence Erlbaum.

GARNER, R. (1987). *Metacognition and reading comprehension.* Norwood, NJ: Ablex Publishing Co.

GARNER, R. (1988). Verbal-report data on cognitive and metacognitive strategies. In C.E. Weinstein, E.T. Goetz, & P.A. Alexander, (Eds.), *Learning and study strategies: Issues in assessment, instruction, and evaluation* (pp. 63–76). New York: Academic Press.

GARNER, R., & ALEXANDER, P.A. (1989). Metacognition: Answered and unanswered questions. *Educational Psychologist, 24*(2), 143–158.

GOBBO, C. & CHI, M. (1986). How knowledge is structured and used by expert and novice children. *Cognitive Development, 1,* 227–237.

GREEN, B.F., MCCLOSKEY, M., & CARRAMAZZA, A. (1985). The relation of knowledge to problem solving, with examples from kinematics. In S.F. Chipman, J.W. Segal, & R. Glaser (Eds.), *Thinking and learning skills, Vol. 2: Research and open questions* (pp. 127–140). Hillsdale, NJ: Lawrence Erlbaum.

HUNTER-BLANKS, P., GHATALA, E.S., PRESSLEY, M., & LEVIN, J.R. (1988). Comparison of monitoring during study and during testing on a sentence-learning task. *Journal of Educational Psychology, 80*(3), 279–283.

KIEWRA, K.A. (1988). Cognitive aspects of autonomous note taking: Control processes, learning strategies, and prior knowledge. *Educational Psychologist, 23*(1), 39–56.

KIRBY, J.R. (ED.). (1984). *Cognitive strategies and educational performance.* New York: Academic Press.

KULKARNI, D., & SIMON, H.A. (1988). The processes of scientific discovery: The strategy of experimentation. *Cognitive Science, 12,* 139–175.

LARKIN, J.H. (1985). Understanding, problem representations, and skill in physics. In S.F. Chipman, J.W. Segal, & R. Glaser (Eds.), *Thinking and learning skills, Vol. 2: Research and open questions* (pp. 141–160). Hillsdale, NJ: Lawrence Erlbaum.

LARKIN, J.H., REIF, F., CARBONELL, J., & GUGLIOTTA, A. (1988). FERMI: A flexible expert reasoner with multi-domain inferencing. *Cognitive Science, 12,* 101–138.

LARKIN, J.H., MCDERMOTT, J., SIMON, D.P., & SIMON, H.A. (1980). Models of competence in solving physics problems. *Cognitive Science, 4,* 317–345.

LESGOLD, A.M. (1984). Acquiring expertise. In J.R. Anderson & S.M. Kosslyn (Eds.), *Tutorials in learning and memory: Essays in honor of Gordon Bower* (pp. 31–60). San Francisco: Freeman.

LOCKE, E.A., SHAW, K.N., SAARI, L.M., & LATHAM, G.P. (1981). Goal setting and task performance: 1969–1980. *Psychological Bulletin, 90*(1), 125–152.

MEANS, M.L., & VOSS, J.F. (1985). Star wars: A developmental study of expert and novices' knowledge structures. *Journal of Memory & Language, 24,* 746–757.

MCCOMBS, B.L. (1989). Self-regulated learning and academic achievement: Phenomenological view. In B.J. Zimmerman, & D.H. Schunk (Eds.), *Self-regulated learning and academic achievement: Theory, research and practice* (pp. 51–82). New York: Springer-Verlag.

MCCOMBS, B.L. (1988). Motivational skills training: Combining metacognitive, and affective learning strategies. In C.E. Weinstrein, E.T. Goetz, & P.A. Alexander, (Eds.), *Learning and study strategies: Issues in assessment, instruction, and evaluation* (pp. 141–169). New York: Academic Press.

MUIR, J., MASTERSON, D., WIENER, R., LYON, K., & WHITE, J. (APRIL, 1989). *Training and transfer of an organizational strategy in gifted and high-average nongifted children.* Poster presented at the meeting of the Society for Research in Child Development, Kansas City, Missouri.

NICKERSON, R.S., PERKINS, D.N., & SMITH, E.E. (1985). *The teaching of thinking.* Hillsdale, NJ: Lawrence Erlbaum.

NOEL, L., & LEVITZ, R. (EDS.). (1982). *How to succeed with academically underprepared students.* Iowa City: American College Testing Service, National Center for Advancing Educational Practice.

PARIS, S.G., LIPSON, M.Y., & WIXSON, K.K. (1983). Becoming a strategic reader. *Comtemporary Educational Psychology, 8,* 293–316.

PARIS, S., CROSS, D., & LIPSON, M. (1984). Informed strategies for learning: A program to improve children's reading awareness and comprehension. *Journal of Educational Psychology, 76*, 1239-1252.

PERKINS, D.N., & SALOMON, G., (1989). Are cognitive skills context-bound? *Educational Researcher, 18*(1) 16-25.

PERKINS, D.N., & SIMMONS, R. (1988). Patterns of misunderstanding: An integrative model for science, math and programming. *Review of Educational Research, 58*(3), 303-326.

PINTRICH, P.R. (1988). A process-oriented view of student motivation and cognition. In J.S. Stark & L.A. Mets (Eds.), *Improving teaching and learning through research* (pp. 65-80). (New directions for institutional research, No. 57). San Francisco: Jossey-Bass.

PINTRICH, P.R. (March, 1989). *Motivational dynamics of self-efficacy and self-regulated learning.* Paper presented at the annual meeting of the American Educational Research Association convention, San Francisco.

PINTRICH, P.R., MCKEACHIE, W.J., SMITH, D.A.F., DOLIJANAC, R., LIN, YI-GUANG, NAVEH-BENJAMIN, M., CROOKS, T., & KARABENICK, S. (1988). *Motivated strategies for learning questionnaire* (MSLQ). National Center for Research to Improve Post-secondary Teaching and Learning (NCRIPTAL), School of Education, The University of Michigan.

POSNER, M.I. (1988). Introduction: What is it to be an expert? In M.T.H. Chi, R. Glaser, & M.J. Farr (Eds.), *The nature of expertise* (xxix-xxxvi). Hillsdale, NJ: Lawrence Erlbaum.

PRESSLEY, M., & LEVIN, J.R. (EDS.). (1983A). *Cognitive strategy research: Educational applications.* New York: Springer-Verlag.

PRESSLEY, M., & LEVIN, J.R. (EDS.). (1983B). *Cognitive strategy research: Psychological foundations.* New York: Springer-Verlag.

PRESSLEY, M., SYMONS, S., MCDANIEL, M.A., SNYDER, B.L., & TURNURE J.E. (1988). Elaborative interrogation facilitates acquisition of confusing facts. *Journal of Educational Psychology, 80*(3), 268-278.

RECHT, D.R., & LESLIE, L. (1988). Effect of prior knowledge on good and poor readers' memory of text. *Journal of Educational Psychology, 80*(1), 16-20.

SALOMON, G., & PERKINS, D.N. (1989). Rocky roads to transfer: Rethinking mechanisms of a neglected phenomenon. *Educational Psychologist, 24*(2), 113-142.

SCHMECK, R.R. (1983). Learning styles of college students. In R. Dillon & R. Schmeck (Eds.), *Individual differences in cognition* (pp. 233-279). New York: Academic Press.

SCHMECK, R.R. (1988). (Ed.) *Learning strategies and learning styles.* New York: Plenum.

SIEGLER, R.S., & JENKINS, E.A. (1989). *How children discover new strategies.* Hillsdale, NJ: Lawrence Erlbaum.

SHRAGER, L., & MAYER, R.E. (1989). Note-taking fosters generative learning strategies in novices. [Brief Report]. *Journal of Educational Psychology, 81*(2), 263-264.

SVENSSON, L. (1977). On qualitative differences in learning: III—study skill and learning. *British Journal of Educational Psychology, 47*, 233-243.

SWING, S.R., STOIBER, K.C., & PETERSON, P.L. (1988). Thinking skills versus learning time: Effects of alternative classroom-based interventions on students' mathematics problem solving. *Curriculum & Instruction, 5*(2), 123-191.

SWING, S., & PETERSON, P. (1988). Elaborative and integrative thought processes in mathematics learning. *Journal of Educational Psychology, 80*(1), 54-66.

VOSNIADOU, S., PEARSON, P.D., & ROGERS, T. (1988). What causes children's failures to detect inconsistencies in text? Representation versus comparison difficulties. *Journal of Educational Psychology, 80*(1), 27-39.

VOSS, J.F., BLAIS, J., MEANS, M.L., GREENE, T.R., & AHWESH, E. (1986). Informal reasoning and subject matter knowledge in the solving of economics problems by naive and novice individuals. *Cognition and Instruction, 3*(4), 369-302.

WEINSTEIN, C.E., & MAYER, R.E. (1986). The teaching of learning strategies. In M.C. Wittrock (Ed.), *Handbook of research on teaching* (3rd ed.) (pp. 315-327). New York: Macmillan.

WEINSTEIN, C.E., & UNDERWOOD, V.L. (1985). Learning strategies: The *how* of learning. In J. Segal, S. Chipman, & R. Glaser (Eds.), *Relating instruction to basic research* (pp. 241-258). Hillsdale, NJ: Lawrence Erlbaum.

WEINSTEIN, C.E., GOETZ, E.T., AND ALEXANDER, P.A. (1988). (Eds.). *Learning and study strategies: Issues in assessment, instruction, and evaluation.* New York: Academic Press.

WEINSTEIN, C.E., & PALMER, D.R. (1990). *The learning and study strategies inventory—high school version.*Clearwater, FL: H & H Publishing Company.
WEINSTEIN, C.E., SCHULTE, A.C., & PALMER, D.R. (1987). *The learning and study strategies inventory* (LASSI). Clearwater, FL: H & H Publishing Company.
WITTROCK, M.C. (1986). Students' thought processes. In M.C. Wittrock (Ed.), *Handbook of research on teaching* (3rd ed.) (pp. 297–314). New York: Macmillan.
WITTROCK, M.C. (1990). Generative processes of comprehension. *Educational Psychologist, 24,* 345–376.
ZIMMERMAN, B.J., & SCHUNK, D.H. (1989). (Eds.). *Self-regulated learning and academic achievement: Theory, research and practice.* New York: Springer-Verlag.

SIX

THE DEFINITION AND MEASUREMENT OF PRIMARY MOTIVATIONAL PROCESSES

Barbara L. McCombs

In this chapter, Barbara L. McCombs develops reasons to measure more than competencies, intellectual abilities, learning strategies, metacognitive processes, and knowledge, in our attempts to improve instruction through an increased understanding of human thought processes. Motivation, especially attribution processes, has become the focus of much research on cognition lately because it sometimes explains more variance in achievement in schools than does any other variable. For this reason, McCombs argues that attribution and self-esteem, including student evaluations of their competencies and abilities, need to be carefully measured, monitored, and related to school achievement. From her research over the last 15 years on the measurement of student motivation and self-esteem, she draws implications for the improvement of educational testing through the measurement of student attributional processes and self-esteem.

Recent concerns about excellence in education have focused attention on student development of their potential abilities and their motivation to engage in self-directed learning. The development of human potential is a topic that has long fascinated humanistic and developmental psychologists, educators, theologians, historians, philosophers, and the "man on the street." Despite this fascination, however, experimental and cognitive psychologists have had difficulty operationalizing and "demystifying" this phenomenon as well as defining and measuring its underlying motivational and intellectual components. In addition, although the development of each child's unique capabilities and potential is a frequently stated goal of American schooling, teachers are often at a loss as to how best to contribute to and enhance this development. Not only is the concern with how to define and measure resident talents and unique capabilities, but it is also with how to support and enhance students' inherent goals or motivations to personally contribute to their own optimal development.

This chapter focuses on recent theoretical and empirical progress in the definition and measurement of what can be referred to as primary motivational processes, that is, those self-system processes that underlie individuals' abilities to generate the motivation necessary for the development of their unique capabilities and potentials, including the intrinsic motivation to learn. The emphasis on these types of motivational processes is stressed because of the tacit assumption that human behavior is basically motivated by the recognition of inherent propensities for self-determination and self-development as well as the desire to achieve a sense of competency in the achievement of personal development goals. In the school context from kindergarten through high school and beyond, students attempt to reach self-development goals in a variety of positive and negative ways, depending on the degree of socioemotional support afforded or denied. If the basic motivational processes associated with these strivings can be assessed and understood—in combination with the assessment and understanding of each student's basic intellectual, physical, emotional, and social strengths and capabilities—educators will be in a better position to contribute to and enhance the unique development of each student. They will be able to help students capitalize on their strengths and minimize their weaknesses.

The first section of this chapter briefly reviews pertinent findings from many subdisciplines of psychology that converge on a better understanding of primary motivational processes and their relationships to the generation of motivation to learn, grow, and develop. A preliminary causal model based on an integration of available research is presented, which specifies the relationships between the identified motivational processes and suggests areas of assessment and intervention. The chapter concludes with a discussion of implications for research on testing in the area of motivational processes critical to optimal learning and human development.

RESEARCH ON PRIMARY MOTIVATIONAL PROCESSES

It is becoming increasingly clear from work in the areas of developmental, social, and cognitive psychology that students' evaluations of their personal competencies, the importance they attach to these competencies, the personal significance they attach to particular learning tasks, and the ways in which these evaluations are used in the differential processing of information are critical determinants of motivation to learn and learning itself. It is known, for example, that negative self-evaluations can create significant barriers to motivation and learning. The specific relationships between these personal evaluations and the underlying processes involved are also becoming more well understood from integrations of research on the self-system and self-regulated learning (McCombs, 1984, 1986, 1988, 1989). From this work, the following general principles relevant to the assessment of primary motivational processes can be defined.

1. *The self-system operates as the base set of "filters" through which all information is processed, transformed, and encoded.* Prevalent theories of the self emphasize the structural and functional nature of self-system variables. From a *structural* standpoint, the self has been viewed as a compound set of multiple, hierarchically organized cognitive structures or schemata that exert a powerful influence on attention, the organization and categorization of information, recall, and judgments about others. (Eccles, 1983; March, Parker, & Barnes, 1985; Paris & Cross, 1983; Pervin, 1985; Rogers, Kuiper, & Kirker, 1977; Shavelson & Bolus, 1982; Shavelson, Hubner, & Stanton, 1976). There is a growing consensus that the organization of the self-system structure is not only hierarchical, but self-enhancing in the sense that one's more positive and central traits or attributes are presented initially at the core, branching out to salient subschemata, and with less positive characteristics represented in the outer ring (Connell & Ryan, 1984; Harter, 1986a; Rogers, Kuiper, & Kirker, 1977). As individuals develop from infancy into adulthood, they see themselves as a locus of causality and engage in a progressively higher-order synthesis of their self-constructed self-views, with a reciprocal coordination and integration of processes used to construct these self-views (Connell & Ryan, 1984).

For the preceding reasons, the self has come to be conceived as an extremely active and powerful agent in the organization of reality and the processing of personal data. In the view of Rogers, Kuiper, & Kirker, (1977), the self acts as the background or setting against which new information, prior experiences, and knowledge are organized into personal schema. Similarly, in Bandura's (1977) self-efficacy theory it is implied that the self is a central processor of efficacy information—a processor that also weighs and integrates diverse information about one's capabilities and regulates choice behavior and effort expenditure accordingly. Further, the nature of the self-structure has been described by Markus and Sentis (1982) as the largest and most available structure or set of structures in memory and as the central and first structure through which all information flows.

Those addressing the self and self-system from a developmental perspective generally agree that one's judgments about the self are both global and domain specific. In Harter's (1986a) work, for example, five self-domains have been found to be relevant in preadolescent and adolescent learners: scholastic competence, athletic competence, social competence, social acceptance, physical appearance, and behavior/conduct. A sense of global self-esteem or self-worth is said to emerge about mental age eight and is operationalized and measured with reference to discrepancy between domain-specific judgments and attitudes about the importance of success in each domain. Harter (1986b) contends that global self-concept is not the sum total of all the evaluations that are made about the self. Rather, it is a function of how important students view these different domains and/or doing well in these domains. For example, two students could have similar perceptions of being low in scholastic ability, but one might think being a good scholar was very important and the other might discount its importance entirely. As a result, one student would think less of him- or herself for not being a scholar while the other would be perfectly happy with the way he or she was. To help students achieve higher levels of self-worth, Harter maintains that it is necessary either to help them discount the importance of specific domains where their competence and importance rating are highly discrepant, or to help them become more competent in those domains. Since ability to do the latter is sometimes limited, her recent research (Harter, 1987) focuses on helping students not only discount the importance of specific domains but also maintain their perceptions of self-worth by getting strong support from their significant others, particularly parents.

From a *functional* standpoint, a number of processes operative in the self-system have been identified. There is widespread agreement that the most important process is self-evaluation, particularly as it relates to one's judgments of personal control and competence (self-efficacy) in general and in specific situations (e.g., Baird & White, 1982, 1984; Bandura, 1977, 1982; Connell & Ryan, 1984; Covington, 1985; Harter, 1982, 1985; Harter & Connell, 1984; Maehr, 1985; Oka & Paris, 1985; Schunk, 1984; Showers & Cantor, 1985; Wang, 1983; Wang & Lindvall, 1984; Wang & Peverly, 1985; Zimmerman, 1985; Zimmerman & Pons, 1986). Self-evaluations are also cited as important as they relate to (a) understanding of the self and the learning task (Baird & White, 1982, 1984; Connell & Ryan, 1984); (b) learning outcomes (Bandura, 1977; Wang & Lindvall, 1984); (c) one's own and others' expectations (Eccles, 1983; Schunk, 1984); (d) the importance of the task and of doing well (Eccles, 1983; Harter, 1986a; Showers & Cantor, 1985); and (e) the cost or effort required (Eccles, 1983; Paris, Newman, & Jacobs, 1985).

In addition to self-evaluation processes, Harter (1982) lists two other self-system processes important to self-regulated learning: self-observation and self-reward. She further contends that all three of these self-system processes require attending to self as an active agent in engaging these processes and as an object or cognitive construction to which these processes are applied. Connell and Ryan (1984) identify a slightly different set of self-system processes in achievement-related behavior: specific and global self-evaluations, processes for coping with anxiety, processes for understanding locus of control for successes and failures, and motivational processes for initiating and sustaining goal-directed and task-involved activity. Connell and Ryan contend that these processes are in support of one's striving to be competent and self-determined. Still other self-system processes that are metacognitive in nature include self-perception or self-awareness (Eccles, 1983; Schunk, 1984) and self-monitoring and checking (Wang & Lindvall, 1984; Zimmerman & Pons, 1986).

2. *The self-referent nature of the self-system's filtering process serves the purpose of maintaining illusions of control or self-determination that lie at the base of self-esteem maintenance.* What seems clear is that the self-system is the initial referent against which knowledge and experience are organized. As the development process proceeds and more complex cognitive structures and knowledge bases are defined, the self-system plays an increasingly active and powerful role in monitoring and orchestrating all mental, emotional, and physical activity. When viewed in this light, one realizes that every decision has a self-referent focus to a greater or lesser (conscious or unconscious) degree. One can then begin to examine the relationships between self-views (self-concept, self-image) and self-judgments or beliefs (self-esteem, self-worth, self-efficacy, self-control) as these relate to perceptions (of the task, or others, etc.), goals (self-protection, self-enhancement), motivation (intrinsic, extrinsic), the use of self-regulated learning strategies, and attributions of causes of learning outcomes. To better understand these potential relationships, however, it is necessary to more fully understand what has been termed the self-serving bias.

The recognition is growing among those concerned with self-system processes that there is an inherent need for individuals to establish and maintain a positive self-image and sense of self-worth. A strong proponent for this position is Covington (1985) who distinguishes between the perceptual bias in one's privately held beliefs about the self and the descriptive distortion in one's public image. He argues that there is a striving to maintain both images, to have them be internally consistent with one another, and to be credible in the eyes of others. In Covington's framework, self-perceptions of competency are said to be the dominant manifestation of the self-worth motive in the classroom achievement context. Similarly, Tesser and Campbell (1982) present a self-evaluation maintenance model which posits that individuals are basically motivated to maintain a positive self-evaluation. The processes of reflection and comparison are said to effect self-evaluations as a function of particular social circumstances. Tesser and Campbell (1982) found that people with high self-esteem maintain positive evaluations of themselves primarily through cognitive perceptual behavior such as perceiving the world in a self-serving way. On the other hand, people with low self-esteem rely more on behavioral strategies (e.g., negative feedback) in their self-evaluations, with the effect that their evaluations are more accurate but not more adaptive.

Mineka and Henderson (1985) discuss the importance of individuals' control experiences and personal beliefs in the development of a positive self-identity. Findings are presented in support of the fact that beliefs about one's intelligence (ability) as stable versus growing differentiate external and internal orientations, respectively, and effect persistence. They maintain that perceptions of control are often inaccurate illusions that help to maintain self-esteem. Harter (1986a) has also found a self-serving bias in high self-worth students. These students tend to slightly exaggerate their competence or adequacy, whereas low self-worth students judge themselves more harshly than even their teachers. As part of this process, high self-worth students—unlike low self-worth students—take more responsibility for their successes than for their failures. Marsh, Cairns, Relich, Barnes, and DeBus (1984) similarly report a positive correlation between the tendency to internalize responsibility and self-concept, particularly when the locus of responsibility is ability versus effort. This finding is taken to imply that attributes are more positively evaluated than behaviors, again indicating the presence of a self-serving bias or attempt to enhance and protect self-esteem. Marsh (1986) more recently reports evidence, however, that this bias is not an intentional distortion of attributions, but is a logical and reasonable way in which students infer causality for their successes and failures that is consistent with their abilities and achievements.

The relationship between the self-serving bias and attributions is further delineated by Cohen, Dowling, Bishop, and Maney (1985). They point out that when students are in a state of self-focused attentiveness (i.e., in ego-involving situations), causal attributions will be made to characteristics of the self and that protection of one's self-esteem has major effects on the types of causal attributions made. Oka and Paris (1985) discuss this type of phenomena in terms of the concept of adaptive motivation, in which personal perceptions and effort are balanced in order to preserve self-worth. They argue that students will choose to engage in and pursue activities that permit them a feeling of efficacy and control and that fulfill their needs, goals, and values. In this way, motivation involves more than mere cognitive competence and may serve the function of preserving self-worth (Oka & Paris, 1985). The role of the self in this framework is to integrate one's expectancies or beliefs about existence, competence, and control into decisions and plans for actions (Paris & Cross, 1983). McClelland (1985) points out, however, that individuals' beliefs that they will be successful will not lead to their engaging in particular tasks or behaviors. In this view, to engage in activities, individuals need to be motivated and interested in the sense that they value the activity and it satisfies some personal motive (e.g., self-enhancement). In fact, McClelland argues that values are more strongly related to choices made than to the actual outcomes of the decisions. In his model, values directly influence the self-evaluation process that then calls into play self-beliefs, which, in turn, give rise to motives and action.

3. *Self-reference can become an effective strategy for generating motivation to learn and for producing more effective learning.* For effective learning, students need to generate motivation to learn and be able to regulate their learning toward personally meaningful goals. Scheier and Carver (1983), for example, have argued that self-focus is the beginning of self-regulation. In their view, it is first necessary to compare what we bring to a task (perceptions of our skills and knowledge competencies) with what's required (standards or goals). We next have to judge whether there are discrepancies between what we bring and what is required, and to make decisions about whether or not to engage in an activity, what level of effort we will exert, and so on. Self-focus is said to engage a feedback loop which is the basic unit of cybernetic control. Harter (1982) makes a similar point and argues that young children do not yet have the skills required for self-attention, that is, the skills required for self-evaluation and self-observation.

In early work by Rogers et al. (1977), self-reference is described as the process of involving the self schema in information processing (e.g., relating content and activities to self-goals). To the extent that a self-reference can be maintained while learning, it is said to be an encoding strategy that results in more enduring and retrievable memory traces (Rogers, Kuiper, & Kirker, 1977; Schmeck & Meier, 1984). Rogers et al. point out, however, that self-reference works as an encoding strategy only to the extent that the learner's self-identity is a uniform, well-structured concept. When it is, it assists in organizing our information and prior knowledge and experience into more highly retrievable subschemata. Schunk (1984) has suggested that the nature of cognitive processing in self-efficacy appraisals may be the same as in processing instructional information.

The preceding theorizing is related to findings reported by Watkins (1984) and Schmeck (1988) on deep-processing approaches that contribute to students' sense of mastery and ability to be effective self-regulated learners. Watkins (1984) reports that self-esteem and locus of control are directly related to students' perceptions of learning and their motivation to study. This motivation, in turn, influences students' use of self-regulatory strategies and their grades. He also presents evidence that internal locus of control and positive academic self-concept are necessary for students to adopt deep-level learning processes. Schmeck (1988) reports that for those students who do not adopt deep-processing approaches (due to external locus of control and low self-esteem), cognitive restructuring approaches which help them change their perceptions, assumptions, and beliefs about themselves and about learning are most effective. These approaches are said to be effective because of their emphasis on the development of personal identity, independence, and responsibility. These findings are in line with Findley and Cooper's (1983) literature review results which showed that (a) internal beliefs were associated with higher academic achievement and (b) the strength of the relationship increases with age.

The self-referent nature of processes related to motivation and self-regulated learning (i.e., attributions for success and failure) is further described by Eccles (1983). She makes the point that attributions play a critical role in the formation of self-concept of ability, but once these self-concepts are formed, attributions may simply mirror one's self-concept. She also points out that one's self-perceptions, needs, and goals play a major role in the personal value one attaches to a particular task. Variables such as the importance of doing well (attainment value), the inherent and immediate enjoyment expected from engaging in the task (intrinsic or interest value), and the perceived importance of the task for some future goal (utility value) are also cited as contributing to the overall value of the task and whether students will choose to engage themselves in the types of activities (e.g., self-regulated learning processes) that promote task mastery. Other important mediators discussed by Eccles (1983) include one's sex-role identity and values, and the perceived cost of success or failure such as the perceived effort required, the perceived loss of valued alternatives, and what one perceives to be the psychological cost of failure (e.g., loss of self-esteem). The personal value students attach to a task is thus one variable that influences motivation and the use of self-regulated learning strategies. Paris, Newman, and Jacobs (1985) emphasize that for learning strategies to be used (including self-regulated or self-management strategies), learners must also personalize, contextualize, socialize, and temporalize them. In addition, judgments must be made regarding strategy utility and economy. According to Paris et al. (1985), strategies are employed as goal-directed actions only after positive perceptions and evaluations of strategy utility and economy are made.

4. *Affect plays a major role in self-system development, motivation, and the engagement of self-regulated learning processes and strategies.* In discussing the role of affect, Iran-Nejad, Clore, and Vondruska (1981) have stated the "affect (emotional experience) is a consequence of the functional integration among various dynamics of mental functioning" (p. 45). These dynamic mechanisms are said to be awareness valence, attention, an inherent sense of self, and an acquired concept of self. The latter two mechanisms have been shown to be powerfully influenced by affect, in the sense that affect plays an active role in the organization of self-relevant information (Pervin, 1985). Harter (1986a) has found that one's sense of self (including one's perceptions of competence and personal control) mediates affect and determines the extent to which one is happy or sad. The attributions one makes regarding

performance have also been shown to differentially influence one's emotional responses such as shame and pride (Weiner, 1980, 1983). In addition, feelings of confidence and of being in control have been cited as the affective component motivating self-evaluations of understanding (Baird & White, 1982, 1984).

Harter's (1982, 1986a) research on causal relations between self-system variables, affect, motivation, and actual performance indicated that students' affective reactions to self-evaluations of competence are most strongly related to motivation to perform, and it is motivation that most directly predicts actual performance. Similarly, Showers and Cantor (1985) postulate that affect (or mood) is one's use of flexible cognitive strategies (i.e., self-regulated learning approaches). They claim that moods are the affective "tags" to other cognitive elements such as one's self-evaluation or self-esteem. The self (as agent) can choose to maintain or alter moods based on flexible strategies and multiple interpretations. To do so, however, Showers and Cantor maintain that one has to have a relatively complex self-organization that is not easily "damaged." It may very well be that low self-esteem students, whose problems have an early developmental and/or experiential basis, have not developed the cognitive complexity necessary to organize information in such a way that it enhances or preserves self-esteem. Expertise is said to be involved in self-image maintenance in terms of one's ability and motivation to respond to the situation, take control, generate multiple alternatives, and be receptive to change (Showers & Cantor, 1985).

Showers and Cantor (1985) also cite the importance of personal self-goals (which are dependent on developing self-knowledge) for learners' development of what they perceive to be appropriate strategies for processing information and planning how to act in specific situations. These self-goals are said to be primarily directed at self-esteem or self-concept maintenance. In a similar vein, work by Markus and her colleagues (Inglehart, Markus, & Brown, 1987; Inglehart, Wurf, Brown, & Moore, 1987) indicates that "possible selves"—one's self-goals—help both to structure behavior and to energize that behavior. Possible selves also help individuals to persevere toward these self-goals. This work suggests that the very process of working toward valued self-goals itself enhances well-being and positive affect.

An even more central role for affect is identified in the work of Mills (1990; Mills, Dunham, & Alpert, 1988; Suarez, Mills, & Stewart, 1987). This work has shown that negative affect is a signaling device to the self that negative beliefs and perceptions are leading to nonfunctional thinking and behavior. Understanding that the self as agent functions above, or outside of, the cognitive system and is the constructor of the beliefs that make up self-concept, self-image, and conditional self-esteem leads to functional thinking and positive affect. With this understanding, individuals experience personal agency and competency, have deeper insights into healthy psychological functioning, feel a sense of well-being, and are able to minimize external stresses within this more positive state of mind. In this view, a student's affective experience of learning, or any other goal-directed behavior, is a signal or measure of the degree to which he or she is functioning consciously from the level of self as agent, or from within a more limited state of awareness, that is, from within his or her learned cognitive system. The cognitive system, in the latter case, will generate stress and negative affect, due to the assignment of agency or cause to external circumstances or reinforcements (nonfunctional thinking).

A PRELIMINARY MODEL OF THE ROLE
OF THE SELF-SYSTEM IN MOTIVATION
AND SELF-REGULATED LEARNING

The preceding background review points to the central role of self-system variables in enacting a process of understanding of one's personal agency that can result in functional thinking, healthy self-esteem, the development of valued self-goals, positive affect, and motivation to assume personal responsibility for learning and for engaging in self-regulated learning activities. The review also points to the importance of considering developmental and experiential factors that contribute to a learner's ability to engage in the necessary positive self-referent processes and understandings that enhance feelings of self-worth which, in turn, allow for the development of personal responsibility and self-regulation. Understanding these relationships through such an integrative review makes it possible to suggest a causal model that can be used in the identification and design of assessment tools and educational interventions which help learners (a) overcome basic impediments to self-esteem, (b) foster perceptions of personal control for learning, and (c) engender feelings of personal competence that underlie both the development of self-regulation capabilities and the motivation to use self-regulated learning strategies in particular learning situations.

The review has also indicated the correspondence between the functioning of self-esteem maintenance processes and information transformation, encoding, and retrieval. Work in the area of the self and self-processes clearly indicates that the self-referent nature of information processing activities forms a set of filters (self-schemas) that can enhance or deter students' abilities to feel efficacious or in control of their learning processes. Without the understanding of the role of self-as-agent in generating these positive self-perceptions, expectations, and feelings, the stage cannot be set for the emergence of self-regulation processes, or for the generation of intrinsic motivation to engage in these processes. Furthermore, without capabilities for what Sternberg (1986) has called mental self-management and practical intelligence, students are unable to capitalize on their strengths and minimize their weaknesses.

Based on the foregoing, the causal model being suggested here is one which assumes that the self-system is the base set of filters (schemas) through which all information is acted upon. The self is both causal agent and the object of self-system processes, the most important of which are self-awareness, self-evaluation, and self-monitoring. The outputs of these self-system processes are perceptions, self-goals, expectations, and judgments about self-capabilities (control and competence) to perform specific kinds of learning tasks. The global and specific nature of self-evaluations of competence and control reciprocally influence the resulting perceptions, self-goals, expectations, and judgments. If the output of the self-system processes engaged as students begin a learning task is positive, the processes of self-regulation and self-reinforcement can also be engaged during the learning process. Within this framework, the self makes use of and controls the entire set of processing capabilities available (including metacognitive, cognitive, and affective processes)—first directing these processes inward at the self and then outward at the required learning activities.

Schematically, this preliminary causal model can be represented as shown in Figure 6–1. The self-system structure is viewed as the central and the first memory structure through which all information flows. In addition, the self is conceived as the "builder" of its knowledge structures whose "plan" or goal is operating at high level of understanding the self as agent that results in self-esteem enhancement and maintenance. This self-serving bias is functionally adaptive in meeting individual needs to be self-determined and to create a positive identity or self-goal (future possible self). The role of the self-system is thus one of creating and maintaining positive self-evaluations before, during, and after learning activities that contribute to the motivation to employ necessary self-regulated learning processes and activities, including deep processing approaches.

IMPLICATIONS FOR RESEARCH ON TESTING

Based on the preceding conceptualization of motivational process variables important in learning and development, a number of implications for testing can be drawn. First, it is clear that assessments of cognitive competencies and abilities are not sufficient for a complete understanding of process variables that will impact learning and development. It is also necessary to assess students' multidimensional primary motivational processes: self-system processes that consist of students' personal evaluations of their competencies and the importance they attach to being competent in specific domains, including their self-goals and evaluations of the personal significance of specific learning tasks. Further, it is important to assess students' understandings of their self as agent and their evaluations of their ability to exercise personal control over and responsibility for their own learning. In addition, a

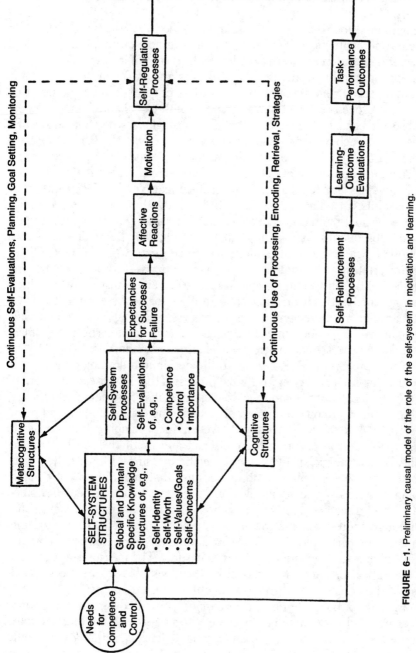

FIGURE 6-1. Preliminary causal model of the role of the self-system in motivation and learning.

Source: From B.L. McCombs, "Self-Regulated Learning and Academic Achievement: A Phenomenological View." In B.J. Zimmerman and D.H. Schunk (Eds.), *Self-Regulated Learning and Academic Achievement: Theory, Research, and Practice.* New York: Springer-Verlag, 1989, p. 63.

developmental focus is necessary in order to identify systematic changes in students' perceptions, self-evaluations, importance ratings, self-goals and values, and intentions, as well as to identify the types of interventions that are most appropriate for students at various ages and stages of development.

In a related vein, research from a variety of sources has suggested that self-system processes need to be assessed as both global and domain-specific variables. It can also be argued that for both global and domain-specific assessments, each variable (e.g., evaluation of self-worth, current and expected self-goals) needs to be assessed as a relatively stable trait variable and as a changing and transitory state variable. Because self-evaluatory motivational processes lead to relatively stable self-concepts and self-identities, they exist as traits. In addition, because these motivational processes can also reflect continual fluctuations in self-evaluations during learning, it is important to subsequently assess the dynamic changes in these processes as a function of different learning conditions and contexts. Comparisons of these changing states with students' trait counterparts—for both global and domain-specific self-system variables—can be extremely instructive to educators concerned with maximizing opportunities for positive student motivation, learning, and development. Thus, it is essential that measures be available to assess trait and state as well global and domain-specific primary motivational processes at different developmental periods.

Some progress has been made in the design and development of measures that tap the primary motivational processes that have been the focus of this paper: global and domain-specific measures of self-concept, self-efficacy, personal agency or control, importance of specific competencies, and possible selves. More work is needed, however, in developing trait and state counterparts and in ensuring the construct and predictive validity and reliability of existing global and domain-specific measures. More analysis work is also needed to ensure that existing measures that might be used are in fact tapping the types of primary motivational processes that have been described here as most directly related to motivation, learning, and development. That is, although there are some measures available, these have to be carefully evaluated in terms of providing a theoretically based, coherent, and comprehensive battery of motivational process measures. The measures must match the theoretical or conceptual model of those variables to be assessed—in terms of the construct and the assessment strategy.

In terms of the preliminary causal model presented here, it is important to bear in mind that much of what needs to be assessed are *internal* belief structures and processes rather than external behaviors. Although one could look at "motivated behaviors" such as persistence, effort, or attention, they only indirectly relate to primary motivational variables as discussed in this chapter. The challenge, then, is to come up with *authentic* and *reliable* approaches to assessing these internal variables that are *nonobtrusive* to teachers and students.

As a starting place in analyzing available measures for their appropriateness, a list of possible self-system measures is suggested in the Appendix. This list is certainly not exhaustive, but represents a set of conceptually consistent measures from which a battery of motivational process tests might be derived as described in the foregoing. The definition, development, and implementation of such a battery is a critical first step in providing educators with the tools they need to maximize student learning and development. Equally important, however, is the use of resulting assessment data in the design and implementation of educational interventions that can further assist each student in maximizing his or her own potential.

APPENDIX:
LIST OF POTENTIAL SELF-SYSTEM MEASURES

Global and Domain-Specific Self-Concept and Self-Worth Measures

1. Harter (1982) *Perceived Competence Scale for Children*—measures global self-worth evaluations and five domain-specific self-worth evaluations (Scholastic Competence, Social Acceptance, Athletic Competence, Conduct, Appearance) in 36-item scale, with 10 importance-rating items.
2. Harter (1985) *Self-Perceptions Profile for Adolescents*—measures global self-worth evaluations (Scholastic Competence, Social Acceptance, Athletic Competence, Physical Appearance, Job Competence, Romantic Appeal, Conduct/Morality, Close Friendship) in 45-item scale.
3. Marsh, Cairns, Relich, Barnes & DeBus (1984) and Marsh (1986) have described the *Self-Description Questionnaire* that yields two total scores (Nonacademic Self-Concept, Academic Self-Concept), and several domain-specific scores (Physical Abilities/Sports, Physical Appearance, Relationship with Peers, Relationship with Parents, Mathematics, Reading, School Subjects).

Other Self-Concept Measures

A listing of some of the most widely researched self-concept measures has been presented by Byrne (1984). These include:

- Bledsoe (1964) *Self-Concept Scale*
- Coopersmith (1967) *Self-Esteem Inventory*
- Piers-Harris (1964) *Children's Self-Concept Scale*
- Barksdale (1973) *Self-Esteem Test*
- Fitts (1964) *Tennessee Self-Concept Scale*
- *Purdue Self-Concept Scale* (Circirelli, Conrad, Crabbit, & Stultz, 1973)
- Sears (1966) *Self-Concept Inventory*
- Gordon (1968) *How I See Myself Scale*
- Soares and Soares (1975) *Affective Perception Inventory*
- Brookover (1967) *Self-Concept of Ability Scale*

Judgment of Competence of Self-Efficacy Measures

1. McCombs (1983) *Self-Efficacy Measure*—measures judgments of competency and control in 20-item scale that has been used with adolescents and young adults.
2. McCombs (1983) *Motivational Skills Testing Battery*—developed for late adolescents and young adults to measure eight motivational areas (career goals/intentions, personal responsibility skills, self-concept, important personal standards/goals, learning performance expectations, critical thinking/problem

solving skills, typical modes of self-talk, success/failure attributions and concerns).

3. Ford and Nichols (1987)—present a taxonomy of human goals and measures of student importance ratings in a number of personal and curriculum domains, including interpersonal competence, personal responsibility and control, and verbal and math abilities.

4. Ford and Ford (1987)—have defined competence motivation as the capability for formulating goals and producing effortful, persistent, and goal-directed activity. Personal agency beliefs are defined as subjective evaluations of one capabilities for attaining desired goals or producing the behaviors necessary for goal attainment, including beliefs or perceptions of competence and control necessary for self-regulation. A recent announcement indicated that his Assessment of Personal Goals and Assessment of Personal Agency Beliefs measures are now available (May 1, 1989, AERA Adolescent SIG Newsletter).

Intrinsic vs. Extrinsic Orientation

1. Harter (1981) *Intrinsic vs Extrinsic vs Extrinsic Orientation Scale*—measures orientation in elementary aged children with respect to five subscales (Preference for Challenge, Curiosity/Interest, Independent Mastery, Independent Judgment, Internal Criteria) in 30 items.

2. Connell (1980) *Multidimensional Measure of Children's Perceptions of Control*—designed to measure, for children 8 to 14 years old, Source of Control (Internal, Powerful Others, Unknown), Competency Domains (Cognitive, Social, Physical), Outcomes (Success, Failures), and Realm of Reference (Self, Others) in two parallel forms of 48 items each.

3. Marsh, Cairns, Relich, Barnes, & DeBus (1984) and Marsh (1986) *Sydney Attribution Scale*—measures student ratings of three plausible causes (ability, effort, external) for scenarios dealing with math, reading, or school in general in which various successes and failures occur.

4. Lefcourt (1982) describes a number of locus-of-control and attribution measures, including:
    *   Bialer (1961) *Locus of Control Questionnaire*
    *   Crandall, Katkovsky, & Crandall (1965) *Intellectual Achievement Questionnaire*
    *   Dean (1969) *Alienation Scales*
    *   James (1957) *Internal-External Locus of Control Scale*
    *   Nowicki & Strickland (1973) *Locus of Control Scale*
    *   Reid & Ware (1974) *Three-Factor Internal-External Scale*
    *   Rotter (1966) *Internal-External Locus of Control*
    *   Mischel, Zeiss, & Zeiss (1974) *Stanford Preschool Internal-External Scale*
    *   Lefcourt (1982) *Interview Questions for Assessing Values, Expectations, and Locus of Control*

Cognitive/Evaluative Appraisal Processes

1. Harter and Buhrmester (1985) *School Concerns Scale*—measures anxieties or concerns in six subscales (Cognitive or Scholastic Performance, Athletic Competence, Peer Hostility/Rejection, Physical Appearance, Behavioral Conduct, Teacher Acceptance) with 42 items.

2. Lazarus & Launier (1980)—have described measures of the emotions generated by cognitive/evaluative appraisals and various coping strategies used to defend against negative appraisals.
3. Mehrabian & Russell (1974)—have developed semantic differential scales of cognitive evaluative appraisal processes and arousal-seeking preferences.

REFERENCES

BAIRD, J.R., & WHITE, R.T. (1982). Promoting self-control of learning. *Instructional Science, 11,* 227–247.

BAIRD, J.R., & WHITE, R.T. (1984). *Improving learning through enhanced metacognition: A classroom study.* Paper presented at the annual meeting of the American Educational Research Association, New Orleans.

BANDURA, A. (1977). Self-efficacy: Toward a unifying theory of behavioral change. *Psychological Review, 84*(2), 191–215.

BANDURA, A. (1982). The self mechanisms of agency. In J. Suls (Ed.), *Psychological perspectives on the self* (Vol. 1, pp. 3–39). Hillsdale, NJ: Lawrence Erlbaum.

BARKSDALE, L.S. (1973). *Barksdale Self-esteem Test.* Idyllwild: Barksdale Foundation for Furtherance of Human Understanding.

BIALER, I. (1961). Conceptualization of success and failure in mentally retarded and normal children. *Journal of Personality, 29,* 303–320.

BLEDSOE, J.C. (1964). Self-concepts of children and their intelligence, achievements, interests, and anxiety. *Journal of Individual Psychology, 20,* 55–58.

BROOKOVER, W.B., ERICKSON, E.L., & JOINER, L.M. (1967). *Self-concept of ability and school achievement III: Relationship of self-concept to achievement in high school* (Educational Research Series No. 36). East Lansing, MI: Educational Publications Series.

BYRNE, B.M. (1984). The general/academic self-concept nomological network: A review of construct validation research. *Review of Educational Research, 54*(3), 427–456.

CICIRELLI, V.G., CONRAD, R.T., CRABILL, C.M., & STULTZ, W.F. (1973). *Purdue instrumentation project progress report: Revision of Purdue Self-Concept Scale* (U.S. Office of Economic Opportunity Contract No. 63655). Lafayette, IN: Purdue University.

COHEN, J.L., DOWLING, N., BISHOP, G., & MANEY, W.J. (1985, December). Causal attributions: Effects of self-focused attentiveness and self-esteem feedback. *Personality and Social Psychology Bulletin, 11*(4), 369–378.

CONNELL, J.P. (1980). *A multidimensional measure of children's perceptions of control.* Denver: University of Denver.

CONNELL, J.P., & RYAN, R.M. (1984). A developmental theory of motivation in the classroom. *Teacher Education Quality, 11*(4), 64–77.

COOPERSMITH, S. (1967). *The antecedents of self-esteem.* San Francisco: W.H. Freeman.

COVINGTON, M.V. (1985). The motive for self-worth. In C. Ames & R. Ames (Eds.), *Research on motivation in education: The classroom milieu* (pp. 77–113). New York: Academic Press.

CRANDALL, V.C., KATKOVSKY, W., & CRANDALL, V.J. (1965). Children's beliefs in their control of reinforcements in intellectual academic achievement behaviors. *Child Development, 36,* 91–109.

DEAN, D.G. (1969). *Dynamic social psychology: Toward appreciation and replication.* New York: Random House.

ECCLES, J. (1983). Expectancies, values, and academic behaviors. In J.T. Spence (Ed.), *Achievement and achievement motives: Psychological and sociological approaches* (pp. 75–146). San Francisco: Freeman.

FINDLEY, M.J., & COOPER, H.M. (1983). Locus of control and academic achievement: A literature review. *Journal of Personality and Social Psychology, 44*(2), 419–427.

FITTS, W.H. (1964). *The Tennessee Self-Concept Scale.* Nashville: Counselor Recordings and Tests.

FORD, M.E., & FORD, D.H. (1987). *Humans as self-constructing living systems: Putting the framework to work.* Hillsdale, NJ: Lawrence Erlbaum.

FORD, M.E., & NICHOLS, C.W. (1987). A taxonomy of human goals and some possible applications. In M.E. Ford & D.H. Ford (Eds.), *Humans as self-constructing systems: Putting the framework to work*. Hillsdale, NJ: Lawrence Erlbaum.

GORDON, I.J. (1968). *Test manual for the How I See Myself Scale*. Gainesville: Florida Educational Research and Development Council.

HARTER, S. (1981). A new self-report scale of intrinsic versus extrinsic orientation in the classroom: Motivational and informational components. *Developmental Psychology, 17,* 300–312.

HARTER, S. (1982). A developmental perspective on some parameters of self-regulation in children. In P. Karoly & F.H. Kanfer (Eds.), *Self-management and behavior change: From theory to practice* (pp. 165–204). New York: Pergamon Press.

HARTER, S. (1982). The Perceived Competence Scale for Children. *Child Development, 53,* 87–97.

HARTER, S. (1985). *Manual for the Self-Perception Profile for Children*. Denver: University of Denver.

HARTER, S., & BUHRMESTER, D. (1985, November). *Instructions for School Concerns Scale*. Denver: University of Denver.

HARTER, S. (1986). Processes underlying self-concept formation in children. In J. Suls & A. Greenwald (Eds.), *Psychological perspectives on the self* (Vol. 3, pp. 137–181). Hillsdale, NJ: Lawrence Erlbaum.

HARTER, S. (1986, July 21). Feeling good about yourself isn't enough. *Today, 8*(2), 2–3.

HARTER, S. (1987). The determinants and mediational role of global self-worth in children. In N. Eisenberg (Ed.), *Contemporary topics in development and psychology* (pp. 219–242). Cambridge, MA: Wiley.

HARTER, S., & CONNELL, J.P. (1984). A model of children's achievement and related self-perceptions of competence, control and motivational orientation. *Advances in Motivation and Achievement, 3,* 219–250.

INGLEHART, M.R., MARKUS, H., BROWN, D.R., & MOORE, W. (1987, May). *The impact of possible selves on academic achievement: An institutional analysis*. Paper presented at the Mid Western Psychological Association, Chicago.

INGLEHART, M.P., WURF, E., BROWN, D.R., & MOORE, W. (1987, August). *Possible selves and satisfaction with career choice. A longitational analysis*. Paper presented at the annual meeting of the American Psychological Association, New York.

IRAN-NEJAD, A., CLORE, G.L., & VONDRUSKA, R.J. (1981). *Affect: A functional perspective* (Tech. Rep. 222). University of Illinois, Center for the Study of Reading.

JAMES, W.H. (1957). *Internal versus external control of reinforcement as a basic variable in learning theory*. Unpublished doctoral dissertation, Ohio State University.

LAZARUS, R.S., & LAUNIER, R. (1980). Stress related transactions between person and environment. In L.A. Pervin & M. Lewis (Eds.), *Perspectives in interactional psychology*. New York, NY: Plenum Press.

LEFCOURT, J.M. (1982). *Locus of control: Current trends in theory and research* (2nd ed.). Hillsdale, NJ: Lawrence Erlbaum.

MAEHR, M.L. (1985). Meaning and motivation: Toward a theory of personal investment. In C. Ames & R. Ames (Eds.), *Research on motivation in education: The classroom milieu* (pp. 115–146). New York: Academic Press.

MARKUS, H., & SENTIS, K. (1982). The self in social information processing. In J. Suls (Ed.), *Psychological perspectives on the self* (Vol. 1, pp. 41–70). Hillsdale, NJ: Lawrence Erlbaum.

MARSH, H.W., (1986). Self-serving effect (bias?) in academic attributions: Its relation to academic achievement and self-concept. *Journal of Educational Psychology, 78*(3), 190–200.

MARSH, H.W., CAIRNS, L., RELICH, J., BARNES, J., & DEBUS, R.L. (1984). The relationship between dimensions of self-attribution and dimensions of self-concept. *Journal of Educational Psychology, 76*(1), 3–32.

MARSH, H.W., PARKER, J., & BARNES, J. (1985). Multidimensional adolescent self-concepts: Their relationship to age, sex, and academic measures. *American Educational Research Journal, 22*(3), 422–444.

McCLELLAND, D.C. (1985, July). How motives, skills, and values determine what people do. *American Psychologist, 40*(7), 812–824.

McCOMBS, B.L. (1983, April). *Motivational skills training: Helping student adapt by taking personal responsibility and positive self-control.* Paper presented at the annual meeting of the American Educational Research Association, Montreal, Canada.

McCOMBS, B.L. (1984). Processes and skills underlying continuing intrinsic motivation to learn: Toward a definition of motivational skills training interventions. *Educational Psychologist,* 19(4), 199–218.

McCOMBS, B.L. (1988). Motivational skills training: Combining metacognitive, cognitive, and affective learning strategies. In C.E. Weinstein, E.T. Goetz, & P.A. Alexander (Eds.), *Learning and study strategies: Issues in assessment, instruction, and evaluation* (pp. 141–169). New York: Academic Press.

McCOMBS, B.L. (1989). Self-regulated learning and academic achievement: A phenomenological view. In B.J. Zimmerman & D.H. Schunk (Eds.), *Self-regulated learning and academic achievement: Theory, research, and practice.* (pp. 51–82) New York: Springer-Verlag.

MILLS, R.C. (1990). *Substance abuse, dropout and delinquency prevention: An innovative approach.* Miami, FL: The Modello-Homestead Gardens Public Housing Early Intervention Project.

MILLS, R.C., DUNHAM, R.G., & ALPERT, G.P. (1988). Working with high-risk youth in prevention and early intervention programs: Toward a comprehensive wellness model. *Adolescence,* 23(91), 643–660.

MINEKA, S. & HENDERSON, R.W. (1985). Controllability and predictability in acquired motivation. *Annual Review of Psychology, 36,* 495–529.

MISCHEL, W., ZEISS, R., & ZEISS, A. (1974). An internal-external control test for young children. *Journal of Personality and Social Psychology, 29,* 265–278.

NOWICKI, S., & STRICKLAND, B. (1973). A locus of control scale for children. *Journal of Consulting and Clinical Psychology, 40,* 148–154.

OKA, E.R., & PARIS, S.G. (1987). Patterns of motivation and reading skills in underachieving children. In S.J. Ceci (Ed.), *Handbook of cognitive, social and neuropsychological aspects of learning disabilities* (pp. 84–111). Hillsdale, NJ: Lawrence Erlbaum.

PARIS, S.G., & CROSS, D.R. (1983). Ordinary learning: Pragmatic connections among children's beliefs, motives, and actions. In J. Bisanz, G.L. Bisanz, Y.R. Kail (Eds.), *Learning in children: Progress in cognitive development research* (pp. 127–169). New York: Springer-Verlag.

PARIS, S.G., NEWMAN, R.S., & JACOBS, J.E. (1985). Social contexts and functions of children's remembering. In M. Pressley & C.J. Brainerd (Eds.), *Cognitive learning and memory in children* (pp. 81–115). New York: Springer-Verlag.

PERVIN, L.A. (1985). Personality: Current controversies, issues, and directions. *Annual Review of Psychology, 36,* 83–114.

PIERS, E.V., & HARRIS, D.B. (1964). Age and other correlates of self-concept in children. *Journal of Educational Psychology, 55,* 91–95.

REID, D., & WARE, E.E. (1974). Multidimensionality of internal versus external control: Addition of a third dimension and non-distinction of self versus others. *Canadian Journal of Behavioral Science, 6,* 121–142.

ROGERS, T.B., KUIPER, N.A., & KIRKER, W.S. (1977). Self-reference and the encoding of personal information. *Journal of Personality and Social Psychology, 35*(9), 677–688.

ROTTER, J.B. (1966). Generalized expectancies for internal versus external control of reinforcement. *Psychological Monographs, 80* (Whole No. 609).

SCHEIER, M.R., & CARVER, C.S. (1983). Cognition, affect, and self-regulation. In J.M. Levine & M.C. Wang (Eds.), *Teacher and student perceptions: Implications for learning* (pp. 157–183).

SCHMECK, R.R. (1988). Individual differences and learning strategies. C.E. Weinstein, E.T. Goetz, & P.A. Alexander (Eds.), *Learning and study strategies: Issues in assessment, instruction, and evaluation* (pp. 171–191). New York: Academic Press.

SCHMECK, R.R., & MEIER, S.T. (1984). Self-reference as a learning strategy and a learning style. *Human Learning, 3,* 9–17.

SCHUNK, D.H. (1984, April). *Self-efficacy and classroom learning.* Paper presented at the annual meeting of the American Educational Research Association, Symposium on Motivating Academic Work in Classrooms, New Orleans.

SEARS, P.S. (1966). *Memorandum with respect to the use of the Sears Self-Concept Inventory.* Stanford, CA: Stanford Center for Research and Development in Teaching.

SHAVELSON, R.J., & BOLUS, R. (1982). Self-concept: The interplay of theory and methods. *Journal of Educational Psychology, 74,* 3–17.

SHAVELSON, R.J., HUBNER, J.J., & STANTON, G.C. (1976). Validation of construct interpretations. *Review of Educational Research, 46,* 407–441.

SHOWERS, C., & CANTOR, N. (1985). Social cognition: A look at motivated strategies. *Annual Review of Psychology, 36,* 275–305.

SOARES, A.T., & SOARES, L.M. (1975). *Self-perception Inventory (SPI): Composite test manual.* Trumbell, CT: ALSO.

STERNBERG, R.J. (1986). Three heads are better than one. *Psychology Today, 20*(8), 56–62.

STIPEK, D.J. (1985). The development of achievement motivation. In C. Ames & R. Ames (Eds.), *Research on motivation in education: The classroom milieu* (pp. 145–174). New York: Academic Press.

SUAREZ, R., MILLS, R.C., & STEWART, D. (1987). *Sanity, insanity, and common sense.* New York: Fawcett Columbine.

TESSER, A., & CAMPBELL, J. (1982). *Self-evaluation maintenance processes and individual differences in self-esteem.* Paper presented at the Symposium on Functioning and Measurement of Self-Esteem, American Psychological Association, Washington, DC.

WANG, M.C. (1983). Development and consequences of students' sense of personal control. In J.M. Levine & M.C. Wang (Eds.), *Teacher and student perceptions: Implications for learning* (pp. 213–247). Hillsdale, NJ: Lawrence Erlbaum.

WANG, M.C., & LINDVALL, M. (1984). *Individual differences and school learning environments* (Report No. 1984/32). Pittsburgh, PA: University of Pittsburgh, Learning Research and Development Center.

WANG, M.C., & PEVERLY, S.T. (1985). *The role of the learner: An individual difference variable in school learning and functioning.* Pittsburgh, PA: University of Pittsburgh, Learning Research and Development Center.

WATKINS, D. (1984). Student learning processes: An exploratory study in the Philippines. *Human Learning, 3,* 33–42.

WEINER, B. (1980). The role of affect in rational (attributional) approaches to human motivation. *Educational Researcher, 9*(7), 4–11.

WEINER, B. (1983). Speculations regarding the role of affect in achievement-change programs guided by attributional principles. In J.M. Levine & M.C. Wang (Eds.), *Teacher and student perceptions: Implications for learning* (pp. 72–97). Hillsdale, NJ: Lawrence Erlbaum.

ZIMMERMAN, B.J., & PONS, M.M. (1986). Development of a structured interview for assessing student use of self-regulated learning strategies. *American Educational Research Journal, 23,* 614–628.

ZIMMERMAN, B.J. (1985). The development of "intrinsic" motivation: A social learning analysis. *Annals of Child Development, 2,* 117–160.

SEVEN

ASSESSMENT OF MATHEMATICAL PERFORMANCE: AN ANALYSIS OF OPEN-ENDED TEST ITEMS

Kevin Collis
Thomas A. Romberg

Recent advances in the understanding of how children learn mathematics should lead to important changes in the assessment of mathematical performance. In this chapter Collis and Romberg show how current assessment procedures in mathematics learning need to be revised to provide useful information for curricular and instructional reform. Multiple-choice tests measure separate skills in mathematics. The relationships among ideas, and their organization and structure, comprise an essential part of what students should learn in mathematics, according to recent research in cognition. To assess the learning of relationships, structure, and organization, along with the learning of thinking skills (i.e., to reason and to solve problems), requires measuring strategies and processes as well as the number of correct solutions. Collis and Romberg discuss procedures appropriate for assessing the learning of relationships, structures, strategies, and processes that characterize the study of mathematics.

The purpose of this chapter is to develop a cognitive framework for examining open-ended test items and the responses to such items, and then to examine a sample of such items and responses from tests that have been given in several countries. The rationale for developing items and analytic procedures from cognitive theory is based on the fact that in the United States during the past decade there has been a consistent call for new procedures for assessing mathematical performance (e.g., Campbell & Fey, 1988; Romberg, 1988; Mathematical Sciences Education Board [MSEB], 1989; National Council for Teachers of Mathematics [NCTM], 1989; Oakes, 1986). The basis for this call, as summarized by Webb (1987), is as follows. The increasing importance of mathematics in society and a new understanding of how children learn have led to demands for reform in the mathematics curriculum. Current assessment procedures, because they are based on earlier views about mathematics and learning, provide inadequate information about performance and if used will inhibit curricular reform. Thus, new assessment procedures must be developed that better reflect current understanding about the ways in which knowledge is constructed and the mathematics that students should learn. In short, "as the curriculum changes so must the tests" (NCTM, 1989, p. 189).

Although critics claim that there are many problems with current assessment procedures, two criticisms in particular seem to be most frequently raised. First, critics argue that the tests reflect a fragmented view of mathematics rather than a view of mathematics as an integrated whole. According to Webb and Romberg (1989):

> Most multiple-choice or fixed-choice tests . . . are designed to measure independent partitioning of mathematics rather than knowledge and use of the interrelationships among mathematical ideas. These tests are organized based on instructional . . . competencies that reflect a view of mathematics as a large collection of separate skills and concepts. (p. 3)

The second frequently voiced criticism is that current mathematics tests predominantly consist of items requiring factual knowledge or procedural skills rather than items that assess students' cognitive abilities: to think critically, to reason, to solve problems, to interpret, and to apply ideas in creative ways. Campbell and Fey (1988) assert that "current standardized assessments . . . are promoting exposure to procedures at the expense of understanding" (p. 62). According to the MSEB (1989), current "tests stress lower- rather than higher-order thinking, emphasizing student responses to test items rather than original thinking and expression" (p. 68). With their focus on solutions rather than on strategies or processes, the current tests

The research reported in this paper was supported by the Office of Educational Research and Improvement of the U.S. Department of Education and by the Wisconsin Center for Education Research, School of Education, University of Wisconsin-Madison. The opinions expressed in this publication are those of the author(s) and do not necessarily reflect the view of OERI or the Wisconsin Center for Education Research.

"reinforce in students, teachers, and the public the narrow image of mathematics as a subject with unique correct answers" (p. 68).

Critics of current mathematics assessment procedures are consistent in what they propose as replacement for current procedures. Campbell and Fey (1988) argue that "it is essential that testing be reorganized to . . . parallel the new goals of the curriculum: the development of mathematical understanding, the interpretation of mathematical events, and the application of mathematical procedures" (p. 62). Similarly, Oakes (1986) cites a "critical need for better indicators" of educational achievement and notes that "we have fairly good paper-and-pencil measures of the most commonly taught basic knowledge and skills. But we lack adequate measures of children's abilities to think critically, to apply their knowledge, or to solve problems" (p. 34).

The NCTM *Standards* (1989) provide specific suggestions regarding what should be assessed. The seven student assessment standards that focus on the assessment of students' understanding of and disposition toward mathematics are:

1. Mathematical power. This broad standard focuses on the integration of the abilities covered in the other assessment standards. It focuses on the extent to which students (a) have integrated the information they've learned, (b) can apply what they've learned to problem situations, (c) can communicate their ideas, (d) have confidence in doing mathematics, and (e) value mathematics.
2. Problem solving. Students should be assessed on their ability to use mathematics to solve problems. All aspects of problem solving should be covered.
3. Communication. Assessment of students' ability to communicate mathematically should focus on both the meanings students attach to concepts and procedures, and on their fluency in talking about, understanding, and evaluating ideas expressed through mathematics.
4. Reasoning. Assessment techniques should specifically assess students' ability to use various types of reasoning that are fundamental to mathematics (e.g., deductive or proportional reasoning).
5. Mathematical concepts. Assessments of students' knowledge should examine their understanding of mathematical concepts.
6. Mathematical procedures. Assessments of students' knowledge of procedures should determine not only whether students can execute procedures, but also whether they know the underlying concepts, when to apply the procedures, why the procedures work, and how to verify that the procedures yield correct answers.
7. Mathematical disposition. Assessments should seek information about students' attitudes toward mathematics, including confidence, willingness to explore alternatives, perseverance, and interest.

Because the emphasis should be not only on solutions but also on processes and strategies, tests should include open-ended items (also called constructed-response or free-response items), that is, items for which the examinee has to *create* a response rather than select a response from a list.

The National Research Council Committee on Indicators of Precollege Science and Mathematics Education recommends "that a greatly accelerated program of research and development be undertaken aimed at the construction of free-response techniques that measure skills not measured by multiple-choice tests" (Murnane & Raizen, 1988, pp. 6–7). In their recommendations for the National Assessment of Educational Progress (NAEP), a national study group recommended that new methods be adopted for the national assessment of mathematics and science to evaluate problem-solving and higher-order skills. "Open-ended and free-response questions . . . require the student to generate the correct answer, not merely to recognize it. Such assessment items would . . . allow for more reliable inferences about the thought processes contributing to the answer" (Alexander & James, 1987, p. 23).

These calls for open-ended test items have been made with full knowledge that there have been, and are, tests made up of such items or tests that contain such items. For example, the "O" Level and "A" Level exams given for many years in Great Britain are comprised of open-ended test items, as is the second section of the Advance Placement Examination in the United States. In fact, the initial use and objective scoring of such items is credited to Reverend George Fisher, an English schoolmaster. His "scale books," used in Greenwich Hospital School as early as 1864, provided the means for evaluating accomplishments in handwriting, spelling, mathematics, grammar, and composition. Specimens of pupil work were compared with "standard specimens" to determine numerical ratings that depended on the types of errors in performance (Greene, Jorgenson, & Gerberich, 1953). However, there are three practical reasons that such items are rarely administered. First, because of their complexity and the time needed by students to construct a response, only a few items can be used. This, in turn, creates two technical problems — sample selection and test reliability. Second, scoring must be done by knowledgeable humans rather than by machine. Thus, interjudge agreement is of concern. Finally, the selection of standard specimens for scaling lacks conceptual validity. We believe what is needed is a framework, based on an understanding of cognitive mechanisms, that could be used both to help in the selection of appropriate open-ended items and to guide the development of valid scaling procedures.

In the second section of this paper a framework is proposed. In the third section a sample of such items and responses is examined. Many of these come from tests administered in other countries where such items have commonly been administered. The paper concludes with a brief section on implications for practice.

COGNITIVE MECHANISM

It seems necessary in the context of this paper to take a close look at what we know currently of the cognitive mechanism itself before we make an attempt to draw theoretical implications that might be applied to assessment practice in mathematics

At least since the time of Binet and Simon's (1908) seminal work on the construction of a battery of tests to identify the educability of school children in Paris, the concept of intelligent behavior and its assessment has been dominated by achievement in the academic domain. Until the current decade, little attention had been focused on intelligence as it might be displayed in extracurricular or everyday activities. Currently, researchers and theorists such as Sternberg and Wagner (1986), Gardner (1985), and Demetriou and Efklides (1985) are redressing this imbalance by specifying differences between academic and everyday intelligence. In addition, the novice-expert research of scholars such as Chi, Glaser, and Rees (1982) and Chipman, Segal, and Glaser (1984) is casting new light on how we might account for individual high-level competence in performing particular skilled tasks involved in domains as diverse as physics and playing chess.

Cognitive development theorists have also moved, over the last few years, toward a view of development which is compatible with this trend. These new directions are reflected in and influencing recent views on the school mathematics curriculum, on instruction, and on assessment; hence our interest in them here. In particular, we need to examine closely the changed emphasis in cognitive theory because it is likely to have a very significant impact on assessment in both the short and the long term.

Theories of Cognitive Development

During the 1980s, several psychologists (Biggs & Collis, 1982; Biggs & Collis, in press; Case, 1985; Demetriou and Efklides, in press; Fischer, 1980; Fischer & Pipp, 1984; Fischer & Silvern, 1985; Halford, 1982; Monoud, 1985) have put forward developmental models in cognition that are compatible and relevant in the context of school learning. Although the genesis of their models is different and each has a fundamentally different orientation, they have features that mark them as neo-Piagetian. For example, they all regard cognitive development as a series of hierarchical skill structures that can be grouped into sets of levels (for convenience a set of levels may be called a stage of development). These sets of levels incorporate skills of gradually increasing complexity, with a skill at a higher level developing directly from specific skills at the preceding level. The processes of development within each stage are parallel from stage to stage and involve the capacity to cope with increasingly abstract concepts.

There are theoretical differences among these theories. Case, Halford, and Biggs and Collis emphasize the importance of working memory capacity; Fischer downplays this factor; Halford is more inclined to the development stage notion than the others; the Case and Halford views on the age level for the onset of formal operations differ by some years from those of Fischer and Biggs and Collis; the transformation rules for within and between stages differ from theory to theory and, indeed, are worked out more systematically in some than in others, and so on. The differences are highly significant within the science of psychology, but it is the common elements among them that enable us to use their insights as a sound basis for identifying key elements in understanding and competence during the school years. It is this identification that is fundamental to developing rational assessment techniques for both diagnostic and evaluation purposes. Since the Biggs and Collis (1982; in press) formulation is more thoroughly worked out for describing and analyzing children's conceptualizations in a school learning context, their proposals are described in some detail below.

The development and structure of learning. With some reservations, it seems that the neo-Piagetian theorists referred to in the foregoing would agree that there are two phenomena involved in determining the level of an individual's response to an environmental cue: the *mode* of functioning, which is determined by the level of abstraction of the elements utilized, and the complexity of the *structure* of the response within that mode. These two together clearly form the basis for the theoretical stance taken by Biggs and Collis (in press) in the SOLO (Structure of the Observed Learning Outcome) taxonomy which is summarized in Figure 7-1. Let us examine Figure 7-1 in some detail.

Ages at which modes typically appear are shown on the horizontal axis; the modes themselves are on the vertical axis. It can be seen that the modes progress from concrete actions to abstract concepts and principles and, in direct contrast to Piagetian theory, the emergence of one mode does not replace its predecessor. The modes in fact accrue, the later developing modes existing alongside the earlier modes. The implication of this last statement is twofold:

1. as the individual matures physiologically, the mode(s) developed earlier continue to develop on the basis of the increasingly mature physical and intellectual background;
2. as the modal repertoire available increases, multimodal functioning becomes the norm.

Let us take a more detailed look at each of the modes, remembering that in this paper we are particularly interested in the first three.

SENSORIMOTOR (AVAILABLE FROM BIRTH)

The elements involved in this mode are the objects in the immediate physical environment, and the operations on them are concerned with their management and coordination. The environmental interaction skills achieved form the basis for movement to the next mode and lay the foundation for the advanced sensorimotor skills that are learned later in childhood and adulthood

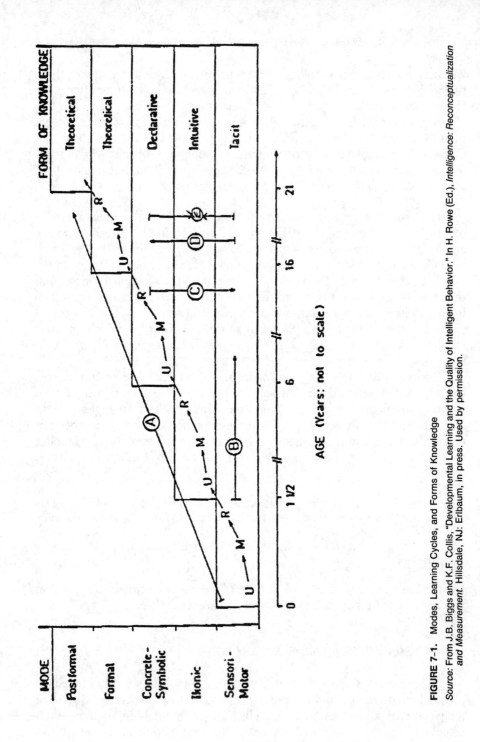

FIGURE 7-1. Modes, Learning Cycles, and Forms of Knowledge

Source: From J.B. Biggs and K.F. Collis, "Developmental Learning and the Quality of Intelligent Behavior." In H. Rowe (Ed.), *Intelligence: Reconceptualization and Measurement.* Hillsdale, NJ: Eribaum, in press. Used by permission.

For example, one indication of the move towards the ikonic mode is shown when the child turns the sensorimotor "understanding" that an object exists regardless of his/her *perception* of it to an ikonic *conception* of it; the sensorimotor skills of walking and grasping form the basis for the running and catching games of later childhood and early adulthood. Most importantly, these sensorimotor skills will now be available to contribute to intermodal activity as the individual moves through other modes.

As indicated in Figure 7-1, the form of knowledge in this mode is well described as *tacit* knowledge because it consists in *knowing how* to carry out an act without necessarily being able to describe or explain it. It is exemplified in sports and other basically kinesthetic activities, such as dance. Golfers can perform a skilled act without being able to describe it in detail, and *know* that they have performed it well because it *feels right*. In fact, introducing modifications to the act by applying the results of information from higher-level functioning may lead, at least initially, to a lower level of performance.

IKONIC (AVAILABLE FROM ABOUT 18 MONTHS)

In this mode the elements become signifiers (words, images, signs) which stand for objects and events; the operations involve the manipulation of these signifiers to establish oral communication, to make links between affect and image [cf. "mythic" stage (Egan, 1984)] and to make perceptually based qualitative judgments. This mode is the first to enable the "internalization of action" which Piaget (1950) defined as the beginning of thought proper and which Bruner (1964) saw as the stage during which the individual formed internal pictures, images, or "ikons" to facilitate this mode of thought.

At the adult level, ikonic thought is not only evident in aesthetic appreciation in the arts and literature but is also well documented for its use by mathematicians and other scientists (Hadamard, 1954). At this level, it is a highly sophisticated form of thought which traces its lineage *directly* back to the early ikonic reasoning of the preschool stage; it should not be confused with geometrical, graphical, or pictorial illustration which forms part of the concrete-symbolic system of representing aspects of the environment. Ikonic thinking leads to a form of knowledge commonly known as "intuitive," which is highly valued by creative thinkers in both the sciences and the arts.

CONCRETE-SYMBOLIC (AVAILABLE FROM ABOUT 6 YEARS)

In this mode, the elements develop from being simply signifiers to concepts that are manipulated using a logic of classes and equivalences, both elements and manipulations being directly tied to the empirical world. This mode enables the concrete world to be interpreted through symbolic systems such as written language and the signs and symbols of mathematics. In the case of the latter, number operations, geometrical diagrams, and graphical representations carried out with paper and pencil and physical models can refer uniquely to real-world happenings. The importance of elementary mathematics stems in large part from the fact that there is a logic and order among the symbols themselves which allow for their independent manipulation either within one concrete representation or from one representation to another. In either case, there is a clear link between the symbol systems and the world. Learning in this mode leads to "declarative" knowledge, which is demonstrated by an ability to make symbolic descriptions of the experienced world, a skill that is virtually a prerequisite for all positions in our society.

FORMAL (AVAILABLE FROM ABOUT 16 YEARS)

The elements in this mode become abstract concepts and propositions and the operations on them are concerned with determining the actual and deduced relationships between them; neither the elements nor the operations need a real-world referent. Development in this mode, which becomes more content specific and increasingly the concern of teachers at the upper secondary and early collegiate levels (Collis & Biggs, 1983), is not of relevance in this paper. Likewise, the postformal level is beyond the scope of this paper and is included in Figure 7–1 for completeness; the reader should refer to Collis and Biggs (1983) and Biggs and Collis (in press) for further information on these last two modes.

A significant aspect of this SOLO model for our purposes is shown in Figure 7–1 by the lines marked A, B, C, D, and E. Line A indicates the development of cognition through the modes or stages from birth to adulthood and was traditionally the major (if not the only) focus of interest in most Piagetian and neo-Piagetian theories. The development is age related and development within each stage is seen as a prerequisite for entry to the next higher stage. It is, however, lines B, C, D, and E which are of most interest here.

Line B represents unimodal learning where the individual uses the characteristics of only one mode while learning a new skill. This is most obvious at the sensorimotor stage where the child has only the elements and operations of that mode available. However, it can occur in any of the other modes. In the concrete-symbolic mode, for example, it appears when a child is being taught the rules for the manipulation of symbols in early algebra without any attempt to link them with some aspect of the child's reality. During at least the primary and early secondary years, instruction aimed at unimodal learning is likely to be counterproductive in the long term.

Lines C, D, and E represent multimodal learning. Line C represents a form of learning which might be called "top down," D "bottom up," and E "two way." The arrowhead points to the basic mode of the skill to be learned and thus to the target for the instructor. For C, we might consider a person who has reached the concrete-symbolic stage of cognitive development setting out to learn a skill such as hitting a golf ball accurately. The skill to be acquired is clearly sensorimotor and it is thus in this mode that the main learning activity must take place. The ikonic mode characteristics of imaging oneself doing the activity and of getting the "feel" for a good hit are helpful adjuncts which improve the efficiency of learning, as is the concrete-symbolic ability to read about how to make a good golf shot. For D, we have the focus on the concrete-symbolic mode where the elements of the basic symbol systems involved in the 3 R's are learned. However, we need to utilize the earlier sensorimotor and ikonic modes in developing these abilities in the concrete-symbolic mode. E represents a focus on the ikonic mode where learning in the creative arts, say, is focused; adjunct modes are brought to bear to supplement and reinforce ikonic/intuitive activities.

Cycles of learning within modes. The other element in the theoretical stance being described is concerned with the structuring of the responses within each mode of functioning. A number of theorists have put forward the notion of an hierarchical sequence of structural complexity as being the hallmark of learning within a mode or stage (Case, 1985; Fischer, 1980; Monoud, 1985). Most see this cycle as not physiologically based and as recurring within each mode. There are usually four levels in a complete cycle; the higher levels subsume the lower in the hierarchy and the achievement of the fourth level signals a move to the next mode of functioning. Figure 7-2 presents a metaphor for the Biggs and Collis (1982) interpretation of this phenomenon. In Figure 7-1 the cycles are represented by the U → M → R symbolism in each mode; the U of one mode represents (in both Figures 7-1 and 7-2) the extended abstract response of the previous mode.

This model has five basic levels in the learning cycle: (1) prestructural, (2) unistructural, (3) multistructural, (4) relational, and (5) extended abstract. Level 1 is below the mode of functioning required for the task at hand, level 5 takes the individual into the mode above that is required, and levels 2, 3, and 4 are the relevant levels in the mode at which instruction in the task concerned should be pitched. If we illustrate this in terms of a particular task, it might make the point clearer.

Suppose a required skill is based in the concrete-symbolic mode (elementary arithmetic, for example). Children operating at level 1 of the learning cycle are still working in the ikonic mode. They might well be able to solve problems within their usual environment by using their highly developed ikonic procedures, but they have not joined in the new concrete-symbolic "game" of arithmetic. Levels 2, 3, and 4 represent the hierarchy of development of the skills in the task concerned in that mode, in this case up

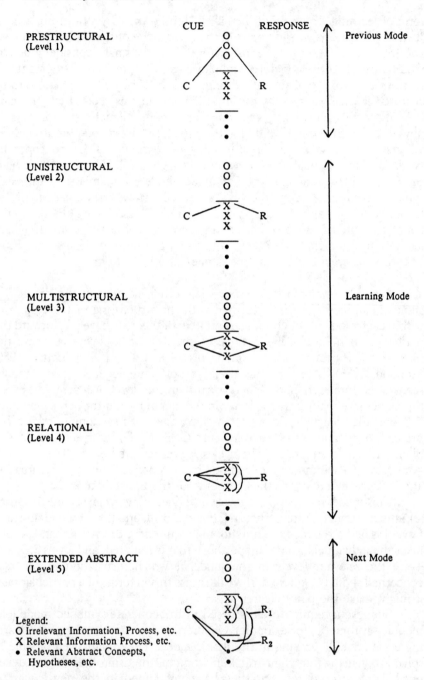

FIGURE 7-2. Metaphor for Learning Cycle

Source: Derived from J.B. Biggs and K.F. Collis, *Evaluating the Quality of Learning: The SOLO Taxonomy.* New York: Academic Press, 1982, pp. 17–31. Used by permission.

to the level of being able to handle generalized arithmetic (Collis, 1975). Level 5 takes them beyond the concrete-symbolic to the lowest level of the formal mode where the abstractions of algebra become the beginning of a new "game" which we might wish to call abstract mathematics.

Implications of Cognitive Theory for Evaluation

There are several obvious implications of the above theoretical position for the evaluation of what a student is doing or is capable of doing in a mathematical topic. First of all, our interest is likely to be centered on an assessment of the level of skill which the child has reached in the topic under consideration. This means that the assessment item must be clearly pitched in the basic mode of the skill concerned and be capable of eliciting the level of functioning within that mode. Second, if, in addition, we are interested in the child's ability to utilize intermodal functioning in solving mathematical problems (e.g., use of the ikonic/intuitive or sensorimotor modes in conjunction with the concrete symbolic or formal modes), then particular strategies for assessing this aspect would need to be employed. An overall evaluation of the child's performance could well take both aspects into account, but the assessor should be able to distinguish clearly between the attempts to assess the former and the items designed to test the latter. An example from outside the field of mathematics might make the point clear.

Children are often taught music in school with the aim of having them appreciate and enjoy it, an ikonic mode aim. Usually these programs incorporate some elementary sight reading of music (concrete-symbolic mode) and some experience in playing a basic musical instrument (sensorimotor). To assess achievement of musical appreciation by assessing the latter skills is to miss the point of the program altogether.

The Mathematical Tasks: Cognitive Characteristics

Let us take a brief overview of the field of mathematics and relate it to the theoretical position outlined above. The model shown in Figure 7–3 seems to give a satisfactory picture. Let us take as an example the area of measurement: the Field A may represent the initial problem of measuring, predicting, or recording a measure of some empirical phenomenon. Consider the typical question that involves finding "How many?" The individual who has to solve the problem has basically two options. One is to use the ikonic mode of functioning and solve the problem by intuition and imaging, perhaps supported by some sensorimotor activity. The other is to translate the relevant aspects to the number field of concrete-symbolic mathematics, operate upon them according to the model which appears appropriate in that field, and then map the result of the calculation back into the empirical field. These two options between them cover the mathematical problem-solving behavior of most people in their everyday lives and, moreover, utilize dis-

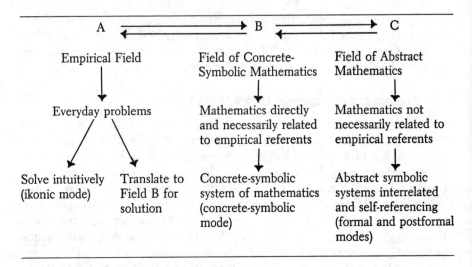

FIGURE 7–3. Overview of Mathematics

Source: From K.F. Collis, *A Study of Concrete and Formal Operations in School Mathematics: A Piagetian Viewpoint.* Melbourne: ACER, 1975, p. 31. Used by permission.

tinctly different modes of cognition, the first ikonic and the second concrete-symbolic.

Mathematics in the ikonic mode.   The characteristics of ikonic mode thinking in mathematics are most easily detected in two areas, one in the literature which describes adults solving mathematical problems in the work place (Scribner, 1986; Carraher, 1989; Resnick, 1987; Hoyles, 1987); the other is both implicit and explicit in the reports of research involving children's first attempts at mathematics when they begin formal schooling (Collis, 1988; Carpenter & Moser, 1982).

Examples of the former come from two sources, the literature on the mathematical tasks performed by unschooled (or minimally schooled) adults, often in developing countries (Carraher, Carraher, & Schliemann, 1985), and the descriptions of basically educated adults performing their everyday jobs in developed economies. Scribner (1986) gives a good example of the latter group. She studied how workers in a dairy carry out their everyday tasks. The striking thing was the irrelevance of the algorithms and other declarative knowledge taught in schools. In taking inventories of stacked milk crates, the workers had memorized short-cut methods of enumeration based on visual imagery. As one worker said, "I walked over and I visualized. I knew the case [of size 16] I was looking at had ten out of it, and I only wanted eight, so I just added two to it. . . . I don't never count when I'm making the order. I do it visual, a visual thing, you know" (op. cit., p. 26). When a stack was not amenable to these methods directly, they mentally transformed array configurations: "When a large array was not a solid rectangle, but had gaps, the men mentally squared off the array by visualizing phantom stacks and counting them" (op. cit., p. 20). Numerous other examples are given of pricing delivery tickets, and other aspects of production. The author found that whereas novices used school-taught procedures, with varying accuracy, experts used highly specific, ikonically based techniques, with nearly perfect accuracy.

Carraher (1988) studied the concepts of addition and subtraction held by 90 adults attending night school who were all normal and competent people in their everyday lives but who had not attended school as children. She found, *inter alia*, that adults with very little schooling (in their first year of night school) could correctly solve addition and subtraction problems, displaying an understanding of the same invariants that define school concepts. However, they used concepts as these applied to specific situations. Their mathematics was a tool for solving problems in meaningful, environmentally familiar situations and was not seen as a culturally developed system of symbols, operations, and relationships which could be applied generally.

Examples of the latter abound, particularly in the numerous studies carried out on the learning of addition and subtraction in the early years of schooling (Carpenter & Moser, 1984, 1983, 1982; DeCorte and Verschaffel, 1987; Peterson, Fennema, & Carpenter, in press; Romberg & Collis, 1987, among others). At a time when the teacher is trying to induct the child into the concrete-symbolic world of mathematics, many of the difficulties that arise relate specifically to the transition from the ikonic mode of everyday language to the concrete-symbolic mode of the language of mathematics. Children's preferred modus operandi is at the ikonic level, as indicated by the facts that (1) the semantic structure of the problems determines the main categories of word problems in this area, and (2) the difficulty of a problem both between and within categories depends upon the semantic structure and children's strategies for solving the problem.

Perhaps this section on the mathematics of the ikonic mode can best be summed up by listing the characteristics of everyday workplace mathematics discerned by several researchers (e.g., Resnick, 1987; Hoyles, 1987) in recent years. In the following summary the workplace characteristic is noted first with the contrasting school mathematics characteristics in parentheses:

1. Done in social context with others present (depersonalized);
2. Procedures adjusted to suit situation (formalized rules, no adjustment possible);
3. Problem embedded in context (problem decontextualized);
4. Social, cultural, and emotional factors are expected to be involved (such factors *not* expected to be involved);
5. Motivation is functional and related to the task in hand (motivation most often related to distant and artificial goals, e.g., grades);
6. Data to be used are not defined and need to be selected for the occasion (data to be used are well defined);

7. Tasks are particular, singular, and individual (tasks are aimed at deriving generalized relations to facilitate transfer);
8. Precision required is defined by the situation (results are expected to be precise and unambiguous);
9. Intuitive reasoning acceptable, for example, the answer is "2." Reason? "I just know" (concrete logic, at least, required).

Mathematics in the concrete-symbolic mode. The concrete-symbolic field (Field B in the foregoing diagram) is the domain in which knowledge is expressed through the medium of a symbol system in a way that makes it immediately available to others without the intervention of its author. It is at the first-order level of abstraction where the symbols of the system can be related directly to empirical referents. It involves a significant shift in abstraction, from direct symbolization of the world through oral language, as is characteristic of the ikonic mode, to written, second-order symbol systems that apply to the experienced world. There is logic and order both between the symbols themselves, and between the symbol system and the world. The symbol systems of written language and signs give us one of the most powerful tools for acting on the environment; they include writing itself, mathematical symbol systems, maps, musical notation, and other symbolic devices. Mastery of these systems, and of their application to real-world problems, is the major task in primary and secondary schooling according to any curriculum theory. Learning in the concrete-symbolic mode leads to declarative knowledge, demonstrated by symbolic descriptions of the experienced world.

The strength and flexibility of the ikonic mode for problem solving in mathematics is clear from what has already been said above, but an understanding of the concrete-symbolic system of mathematics is essential for competent mathematization of the environment, an essential skill in modern life.

Powerful as the strategies of the ikonic mode are for solving a given problem, the inability to communicate the process of decision making directly and unequivocally to others and the context specificity of ikonic mode strategies are perhaps their most serious weaknesses. With regard to the latter: first, they are not generalizable to cover a large number of differing empirical situations; a concrete-symbolic statement such as $6 - 4 = 2$ extracts the "mathematics" out of a variety of semantically different problems that involve such actions as comparing, separating, combining, and equalizing (Carpenter & Moser, 1983). Second, they do not have the versatility to enable new results to be obtained by manipulating the symbols in an existing statement or by converting one representation to another in the same mode. For example, in the first case, if we have $[\ ] + 5 = 8$, we can rearrange the statement by following the mathematical rules to $8 - 5 = [\ ]$. This new statement can be referred to the original problem to provide a different view of it. Likewise, for an example of the second case, let us consider graphical representations. A table of data, already a translation from the empirical field, can be converted to a graph which not only provides a different view of the data but also may show new, unexpected relationships not discerned in the original tabulation. Third, because of the direct links with empirical reality, the results of any process carried out in the symbol system can be validated by reference to the real world. Finally, they do not appear to contribute to the development of "disembedded" thought, which Donaldson (1978) puts forward as one of the most culturally prized outcomes of schooling.

An alternative, but complementary, view of mathematics in a concrete-symbolic system was put forward by Vergnaud (1982) with his notions about "conceptual fields." For Vergnaud, the properties of conceptual fields are:

1. A set of situations that make the concepts meaningful;
2. A set of invariants (rules) that constitute the concept; and
3. A set of symbolic situations used to represent the concept, its properties, and the situations that it refers to.

For example, the related mathematical concepts of addition and subtraction of whole numbers has been defined by Vergnaud as a conceptual field called "additive structure." This field is derived as follows:

1. The symbolic statements that characterize the domain are identified; for example, in the present case, $x + y = z$ and $x - y = z$, where x, y, z are natural numbers;
2. The implied task to be carried out is specified; for addition and subtraction this means describing the situations where two of the three numbers x, y, z (see the foregoing) are known and the third is not;
3. The rules (invariants) that can be used to complete the task are identified (e.g., modeling, counting, routine procedures, etc.); and
4. A set of situations that can be used to make the concepts, the relationships between the concepts, and the rules meaningful is identified (e.g., change, combine, and compare problems).

The result of following through on the foregoing steps is a map of the domain of knowledge.

Mathematics in the formal mode. Although the concrete-symbolic mode is the one in which the higher cognitive aspects of everyday living are conducted and hence is of most concern here, a brief consideration of the higher modes is warranted for two reasons. First, sometimes a mapping from the empirical Field A requires an elementary understanding of part of Field C to facilitate the work in Field B. For example, if a mapping from Field A to B in the area of number operations shows a need for the use of logarithms, the numbers are mapped into Field C by use of the relevant tables, work is done with the new operations and elements appropriate to this field, and then the results returned to the empirical field via Field B. Second, this is the field that must be mastered by those high achievers in mathematics who will aim for a level of skill associated with professional mathematicians. This group of students begins to appear in the school population in the final years of secondary school. Although few in number, they are a very important segment of the school population and must not be overlooked in any paper which purports to discuss curriculum or assessment.

The formal mode is the mode of higher-order abstractions where the symbols and the operations can rarely be related directly to an empirical reality. It is the realm of relationships, theory, and hypotheses where conjectures are tested against the constructs and constraints of the defined field. Thinking in the formal mode then refers to a superordinate abstract system in which any given topic is embedded, and which can be used to generate hypotheses about alternative ways of ordering the world. This superordinate system becomes identifiable with the body of knowledge that currently prevails in a discipline such as mathematics. Professional, as opposed to technical, competence requires an understanding of the first principles underlying the discipline so that the practitioner can generate viable alternatives when rule-of-thumb prescriptions prove inadequate to the particular case. Thinking in the formal mode thus both incorporates and transcends particular circumstances. This mode begins to appear in some individuals, with respect to their particular specializations, from about 14 years of age, but does not generalize to all thinking, and in some individuals may not develop at all. The formal mode is the level of abstraction usually required in undergraduate university study, and some evidence of formal thought in the proposed area of study is usually considered essential for admission to university (Collis & Biggs, 1983).

Mathematics in the postformal mode.   If formal thought is usually the maximum level of abstraction required at the undergraduate level and in professional practice, questioning the conventional bounds of theory and practice, and establishing new ones, is what constitutes postformal thinking. Postformal thought may be seen in high-level innovations in many fields; many of the prodigious performances in music, mathematics, literature, and the arts noted by Gardner (1985) seem to be of this kind. Educationally, it is institutionalized in postgraduate study, and in basic research. Demetriou and Efklides (1985) operationally define postformal thought with tests requiring the respondent to operate in novel systems and, in a metacognition test, to report on their processing while solving novel problems. They found, as did Commons, Richards, and Kuhn (1982), that postformal thought defined in this way was rare even among university students. Nevertheless, some kind of postformal thinking is required in original research. Functioning at this level is not the concern of this paper and, in any case, the method of assessment by peer appraisal is well established and well regarded.

Implications of Cognitive Task Characteristics
for Assessment

Thus far in this section a framework has been drawn which links the nature of the different levels of mathematics with the different modes of cognitive functioning. The final task is to look at the implications for assessment.

In the school situation, three main purposes can be discerned for assessment. One is to determine the student's ability for learning a particular content; a second is to check the student's progress during the learning process; and a third is to measure the level of attainment achieved at the end of the learning sequence. These three purposes need to be scrutinized in the context of the previous points.

From the earlier discussion it is clear that there are two interlinked variables that need to be considered. One is the mode(s) in which the child is capable of functioning in mathematics and the other is the ability to map from one mathematical field to another as appropriate.

The mode (and the level within that mode) at which the child can work clearly sets an upper level on the mathematical field in which he/she can operate. Thus, items need to be devised that can assess mathematically related skills in each of the modes. Although in need of reassessment and reorganization in terms of more recent insights in both cognitive theory and mathematical instructional practice, means of testing in the concrete-symbolic and formal modes are readily at hand because most of the effort at testing mathematics achievement over the past 100 years has been concentrated in this area. The earlier-developing modes are virtually not addressed at all.

The ability to map from one mathematical field to another is obviously closely intertwined with intermodal functioning but must be considered in its own right in this context. It forms an important part of the instructional process at two crucial periods of the individual's mathematical life—at the beginning of doing concrete-symbolic mathematics upon arriving at school, and at the transition into abstract formal mathematics toward the end of high school. In either case, failure to learn the process at the appropriate time appears to make future progress into the higher-level field very difficult.

Moreover, assessment techniques need to cover both diagnostic and evaluative functions. The former is related to the first two purposes set out above and the latter to the third. The evaluative function, which is concerned with the level of attainment, usually involves a series of separate assessments which are pulled together to give a picture of achievement on the topic or course as a whole. On the other hand, the diagnostic function is usually best served by more specifically focused tests which are organized less formally and are seen to be independent of evaluative overtones.

Whichever function is being served, however, the two variables, level of functioning within mode(s) and relevant mapping abilities displayed, are the ones to be assessed. This clearly involves using techniques that will both open up students' thought processes and patterns as they work on a mathematical task to instructor scrutiny and enable them to perform at their optimal level. With respect to the latter, Fischer and his colleagues (Fischer & Kenny, 1986; Fischer & Knight, in press) have shown quite dramatically the differences in performance by individuals tested under the kinds of conditions usually associated with school assessment and those tested on the same questions in a situation providing a high level of environmental support. This support, in the case of some arithmetical tasks, consisted of showing the students a sample good answer and allowing them time to think it over and to ask questions about it before asking them to respond. The results, when compared with those from the usual immediate-answer—without support—technique showed that the students with support functioned at, or near, their optimal level while the others performed at their typical functional level, which was much lower. No longer can assessment procedures be tied to concern with only the product or answer obtained within the traditional assessment environment; the concern must be with the process, regardless of whether the evaluative or diagnostic function is being served.

During the past decade the need for assessment techniques that would open up children's thought processes has accompanied curriculum developments that have been designed to reorient school mathematics towards problem solving, practical mathematics, discussion, communication, and open investigation. The result has been a strong move away from product-oriented tests, such as multiple choice, to process-oriented tests which include *inter alia* projects, extended tasks, open-ended questions, and oral tests. These tests have been largely based on exemplary teachers' intuitive ideas rather than on research or relevant theory. In other words, alternative assessment procedures are being created; the question is, What are they likely to be assessing? In the next section, some examples of the items generated in the light of the theoretical stance taken in this section are examined.

CURRENT ASSESSMENT PROPOSALS: AN ANALYSIS

General Summary of Current Assessment Trends

An outstanding feature of the current mathematics education scene is the rejection of the traditional curriculum and the methods of assessment associated with it. In the traditional view, the curriculum was fragmented into subject areas, such as geometry, arithmetic, algebra, and these subjects further fragmented into topics like notation, numeration, statistics, and so on. Assessment in this curriculum was concerned with the correctness of answers and procedures, the products of the mathematical process as they have been called. Multiple-choice-type items, in many cases, were the vehicle, and, in virtually all cases, whether this format was used or not, the test sought a unique answer that was available by following a procedure that was expected to be known.

Wherever we look in western education systems, this rejection of the traditional paradigm has taken place. There has been a change in emphasis in the curriculum from product to process, from fragmentation and procedural knowledge to integration and problem solving. The basic aim is well formulated in the NCTM *Standards* (1989) by its concept of "mathematical power"; the notion of empowering the students to be able to apply their mathematical knowledge, concepts, and abilities in problem solving, communication, and reasoning. In all cases, it has been realized that sustaining this new set of aims requires the use of new assessment techniques geared to the change in direction.

The techniques settled upon have much in common with one another; they all aim to open the students' process of thinking and working to instructor scrutiny so that they might be evaluated with or without reference to the final product. This kind of evaluation not only emphasizes the interest in the mathematical procedures adopted by the child, but also takes into account the initiative, perseverance, and interest displayed, communication skills shown, and concepts and models of thinking drawn upon. Another feature common to the new assessment is the readiness to encourage the use of tools in mathematics. Calculators and computers are not the only tools; library and workshop resources, as well as people resources from outside the classroom, are expected to be utilized by the student in solving mathematical problems.

It will be clear by now that the task of assessing the processes involved in mathematical reasoning is enormously complex, especially when compared with the traditional product-based assessment. It will be equally clear that it is a task which we cannot fail to carry out effectively without the risk of throwing the whole new thrust in curriculum into jeopardy. Let us look briefly at some recent attempts at devising tests to fit the new paradigm.

Currently, tests and test items are being developed via operational-type research and are based on the intuitions and experiences of good practitioners and mathematics education researchers. From a basic idea, items and/or procedures are developed, tried out, and the results analyzed in various ways with a view to improving them and/or discerning their evaluative relevance. Most items seem concentrated on two aspects that are neglected in tests that were developed using the traditional model. First, they try to ensure that the student opens up the thinking process for the assessor to view and, second, they make provision for the student to show an optimal level of skill by removing traditional constraints such as (a) restricted time, (b) discouraging the use of resources outside one's own knowledge, and (c) limiting the use of tools.

The items devised within these guidelines may be categorized as closed or open. The latter, often called constructed-response items, are of most significance here, as they are far better adapted for testing the new objectives than are closed items, but some mention of the former is warranted in order to put the new practices in perspective.

Closed items, which might include multiple-choice formats, are recognizable as direct descendants of the traditional mathematics test. The response required is clear from the context; there is little, if any, scope for initiative, investigation, imagination, or cooperation, and there is a unique answer. Their main use appears to be in providing an efficient and economical means of assessing knowledge of and ability in routine calculations, procedures, and algorithms. All seem to agree that these skills are still an important part of mathematics education, even if the prominent role they played in the earlier mathematics curriculum has been reduced to a small fraction of what it was. This reduction is represented by less reference to closed items in the curriculum documents, less time devoted to them in instruction, and much less weight being given to them in assessment of the individual's mathematical skills.

In summary, closed items are still likely to form a part of the armory of the assessor, but items are being devised that more readily expose the students' procedures and allow for a variety of techniques to reach the same end. Open items consist basically of items in which the testee has to create a response using whatever resources he/she can bring to bear, hence producing a constructed response. A wide variety are being developed and, although they vary on many dimensions, they all set out to test the higher-order aims of the new curriculum and expose the student's reasoning to view as he or she moves toward a solution. There are variations in time allowed, from restricted-time tests carried out under the traditional examination conditions to projects that might take a semester to complete; in degrees of cooperation and outside help allowed, from none to unlimited; in amount of mathematization of the data required; in amount of writing required, from virtually none to persuasive essays; and so on. All have problems with objectivity of assessment and each has its own particular advantages and disadvantages.

Despite the variety of techniques used to set up the problem situation, the basic format for this type of item is one in which the context is established by a series of propositional statements followed by questions to which the student is expected to construct a response. The nature of the context and the open-ended construction required make demands upon both student and assessor that are different from the traditional form of test item. These two sets of demands are looked at in some detail in the next two sections of this chapter.

The Student's Cognition Task in Assessment Situations

We now turn to a consideration of the task that children face when presented with a constructed-response item; first, we present an analysis consonant with the theoretical stance taken earlier, and then an examination of some actual responses made by children to this type of item.

As was mentioned above, the problem is placed in context by a series of propositional statements, followed by a question that seeks a response. The student needs to take the given propositions and decide on a course of action that might be schematized as shown in Figure 7-4.

The student can immediately proceed down column L or R; at row C, Column L bifurcates and leads in the case of C(i) to an irrelevant conclusion (in the given context) or, in the case of C(ii), to an intuitive relevant solution. The route shown in Column R is traditionally associated with mathematical problem solving. However, it is rare that a student will stay purely on one track [L(ii) or R] if the problem is novel. In this case, there is likely to be movement both ways at either rows B or C or both—this will apply whether the subject is basically following route L or route R. The workplace mathematics literature shows that minimally educated adults solving problems in the ikonic mode utilize any number skills that they have (Carraher, 1988), while the use mathematically competent individuals make of this ikonic mode is well known (Hadamard, 1954). It would appear that the task for the instructor is to find ways of assessing what the individual is doing in rows B and C.

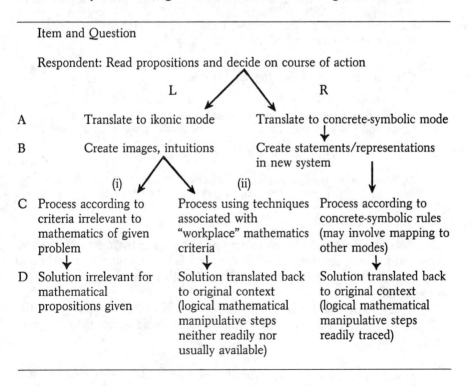

FIGURE 7-4. Possible Course of Action for Cognition Task

Testing at C_L is concerned with the ability to work cooperatively, to handle a particular context, to use outside resources, to define data to be used, to judge degree of precision required, to assess attitude and intuitive ability in problem solving, and to judge flexibility of reasoning. Testing at C_R is focused on knowledge and understanding of mathematical procedures, mathematical concepts, communicative ability with mathematical language, and problem solving with mathematical models.

C_L and C_R together seem to define mathematical power as defined in the *Standards* document. Under the traditional assessment procedures the focus was on C_R abilities in a very narrow range; tests for the new curriculum should be devised so that the assessor can look at both C_L and C_R *and* their interaction.

Let us look at examples of student constructed-responses to problems tried out and analyzed by the California Assessment Program (California State Department of Education, 1989).*

Problem C:
James knows that half of the students of his school are accepted at the public university nearby. Also, half are accepted at the local private college. James thinks that this adds up to 100 per cent, so he will surely be accepted at one or the other institution. Explain why James may be wrong. If possible, use a diagram in your explanation. (p. 21)

Class of responses following $C_{L(i)}$ route:

(a) This may be wrong because there may be other students that are going to junior colleges, state colleges, work full time or take a break (accompanied by a circle graph illustrating some of this statement).

(b) That's wrong because everyone doesn't go to college. I think it's 15 percent doesn't go, 45 percent that goes to local college, 40 percent that goes to private college.

Both students "solve" the problem on the basis of their everyday knowledge and folklore, but they know the question is in a mathematical setting so they both "throw in" some (incorrect or irrelevant) mathematical representations.

This problem lends itself to solution by following route $C_{L(ii)}$ as the following comment (see page 105) from the California Assessment Program report shows.

*Examples presented here are from the author's 1989 report for the California State Department of Education entitled *A Question of Thinking: A First Look at Students' Performance on Open-ended Questions in Mathematics.* Used by permission.

Of the students who succeeded in understanding and solving this problem (20% of the sample), all were able to make a statement to the effect that some students may be accepted at both schools . . . good responses included more complete explanations . . . and diagrams (Venn diagrams, picture diagrams, keyed lists, comic strips, pie graphs, or charts) that clarified the reasoning. (p. 22)

Students who set out along route R "often resorted to meaningless manipulations of symbols" (p. 26).

The type of item just described seems very suitable for use in testing the student's ability to solve problems that require the background experience that enables an image of the essence of the problem to be formulated and which encourages use of those intuitive abilities associated with the ikonic mode of functioning. Let us turn to one in which some successful students clearly used their ikonic skills at certain stages of the solution process, although it essentially focused on the concrete-symbolic mode.

Problem E:
    The square shown below has sides of 2 units. Connect the mid points of the sides of the square, in order, to form an *interior* square. Repeat the same process to make squares within squares.

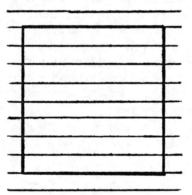

a. Draw the first five *interior* squares.
b. Write the sequence of numbers that represent the areas of the first five *interior* squares.
c. What rule can be used to find the areas of the nth *interior* square? (p. 36)

The assessors' comments speak for themselves. They say, in part,

The (successful) students were able to translate correctly from the verbal description to a geometric figure . . . Students who drew the figures correctly and also calculated the areas of the five interior squares generally appeared to use one of three approaches:

- They used the Pythagorean theorem, found the length of a side and then found the area.
- They counted squares and partial squares on the grid behind the figure.
- They used a "transformations solution" by folding the corners of the larger squares ... This procedure was not demonstrated, of course, but some students appeared to have visualized this process and used it in their solution. (p. 37)

Of the many unsuccessful students (only 1.5 percent of the sample successfully completed the whole problem), "the majority of students were unable to complete successfully step (a) of the problem ..." (p. 38) and showed a lack of ability to map the propositions in the problem into the correct symbolic mode because they could not handle the meaning of concrete-symbolic terms such as *mid-point, square,* and *in order*. Moreover, many were misled by making inappropriate perceptual, qualitative judgments about aspects of the figure — a characteristic associated with the ikonic mode.

This last problem represents a class of problems suitable for use in testing students' abilities: to translate empirical statements into the concrete-symbolic mode; manipulate the resulting symbols of the particular symbolic subsystem according to the specific rules of that system (relationships of the dimensions of a square and the Pythagorean theorem in the foregoing case); and use their experience in the system to achieve any "intuitive" insights necessary (in this case, seeing a number pattern).

The two examples analyzed so far seem good examples of their type. In the first, designed to test in the ikonic mode, the students were given no option but to proceed in that mode if they were to have a chance to succeed. Likewise, the second forced students to move immediately into the concrete-symbolic mode and translate verbal description into a geometrical figure given various geometric constraints.

The third example (Problem A) is not worded so precisely and thus some students followed one track while some followed the other.

Problem A:
Imagine you are talking to a student in your class on the telephone and want the student to draw some figures. The other student cannot see the figures. Write a set of directions so that the other student can draw the figures exactly as shown below. (p. 7)

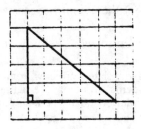 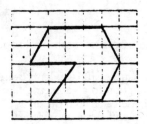

Some students immediately proceeded via the concrete-symbolic process of mathematizing in various ways; others proceeded to describe the image as they would in, perhaps, an art class. An example of the first procedure using the second figure was:

Make points A = (0,0); B = (1,2); C = (4,2); D = (5,0); E = (4, −2); F = (1,−2); G = (2½, 0). Connect the points in alphabetical order then connect G to A. (p. 8)

An example of the second procedure using the same figure was:

Draw a straight flat line with two slanted lines on the side, on right one come down the same opposite side, and on left side make 1 inches inside (each) then draw away from it, (then) now connect both to corners. (p. 10)

Both responses were accompanied by correct representations of the figure.

If we assume that the assessor wanted to test the ability to mathematize a situation and communicate it, the only clues to this intention are: (1) it is in a mathematics test; (2) the drawings given are on graph paper; and (3) the term *exactly* has implications for experienced mathematicians. In other words, the question is not worded appropriately for the purpose envisioned. Even the setting "calling a friend on a telephone to describe the figures" points the students towards the ikonic mode in which most normal oral communication occurs. If, on the other hand, the assessor wished to judge the ability to visualize the situation and to communicate this visualization via the ikonic mode, this intention was not made clear either.

The examples discussed so far, which are examined in more detail in the Appendix, concentrate on testing abilities in either the ikonic or the concrete-symbolic mode. The obvious third type of item is one which sets out to evaluate both modes in one question. The OW & OC publication (de Lange, 1987) gives an example of this in describing what is called the *two-stage-task*. Basically, the item consists of three distinct parts. The first part consists of the item that sets the scene and gives all the necessary information; the second consists of questions that specifically ask the students to mathematize aspects of the information and to calculate various responses, a concrete-symbolic task; the third section asks the students to write extended responses (such as an essay) to explain, to advise, to discuss limits with respect to both the original information (story) and the results obtained in Section 2. To avoid obvious problems such as an inability to get started or incorrect concrete-symbolic work inhibiting responses in Section 3, the assessors devised an interesting way to obtain the responses.

The students were presented with the test initially in a restricted time format in which they were expected to attempt only the questions in Section 2. These responses were corrected for major errors and problems and returned to the students with appropriate feedback. The students were then required to do the *whole* test again at home without restrictions. They could choose to incorporate the whole test in one essay, do the questions in order in the traditional way, or use some combination of these procedures.

This testing format seems ideally suited to the new curriculum:

- It tests all the main aims;
- It can be adapted for use with other procedures such as take-home tasks, interviews, projects, and the like;
- It can be used to test explicitly the students' abilities in both the ikonic and concrete-symbolic modes separately as well as in conjunction—the latter being an important skill usually only tested implicitly;
- It tests what students know, with a little help, and thus allows for optimal performance; and
- It provides for reflection as an important element in the learning process.

The results of the trials (de Lange, 1987) tend to support these assertions; for example, student results in the first stage showed the usual spread from poor to excellent; in the second stage all the students performed satisfactorily; girls performed less well than boys in the first stage but the difference disappeared in the second stage; students performing well in stage one perform equally well in stage two; students performing poorly in the first stage had their self-confidence enhanced when they did well in the second stage, and so on.

The Task for the Assessor

It is never an easy task to translate new curriculum directions and aims into practice. In the past many curriculum thrusts have been stymied because of the failure of either instruction or assessment, or both, to translate new curriculum ideas satisfactorily into their domains. Of these two, assessment has been the least adaptable and, since instruction tends to concern itself mainly with what is tested, assessment has been the target of the major reactionary force. This time around educators have realized the problem and resolved to do something about it—so much so that one hears talk of an "assessment-led" revision of mathematics education. That this is not mere rhetoric is shown in the emphases advocated by researchers and teachers during tryouts of the new testing procedures. Emphases which appear to be common include:

- Assessment is an integral part of learning and the techniques advised highlight this; for example, making arrangements for feedback at all possible stages of the process;
- Assessment aims at finding out what students know rather than seeking out only what they do not know;

- Most testing provides for performance at the student's optimal level by building in the necessary conditions, not simply by exhortations such as "doing your best as this test is important";
- The tests devised appear to have operational face validity vis-à-vis the new aims; and
- Tests are not excluded on the grounds that there is a problem with objective scoring; ways are found to increase objectivity of scoring when this problem occurs.

It so happens that this move on the part of educators is strongly supported by recent research-based theory coming from cognitive scientists and described in an earlier section. The key to this agreement lies in the notion of modes of functioning and its place in mathematics problem solving. The assessor needs to take account of this last concept at two points, at least, in the process of considering a particular item; first, when setting the item and, second, when evaluating the various responses that the item elicits, the latter in order to provide information for future instruction. Let us examine this idea in more detail.

We are assuming in what follows that the modes to be considered are the ikonic, the basis for intuitive thinking, and the concrete-symbolic, the basis for thinking in elementary mathematical systems. Let us briefly recapitulate the characteristics of these two modes for this context.

1. The ikonic mode is *intuitive* in the sense that it provides qualitative insights into a problem structure. These are often perceptually based and/or based on simple analogous reasoning and the outcome is not usually amenable to the straight logic associated with the system of mathematics. Although it may be used at any time during the problem-solving process, we are thinking specifically of its use at the very first stage.

2. The ikonic mode is concerned with forming *images*, visualizations of situations, concrete structures, and arrangements which sometimes lead the individual into making qualitative diagrammatic representations of elements of the problems.

3. *Communication* tends to conform to the oral structure of everyday language. Rather than being propositional, the ikonic mode is descriptive and closely tied to expressing feelings and intuitive and aesthetic associations. It is not basically suitable for precise mathematical communication which requires the concrete-symbolic mode.

4. The ikonic mode is the *affective* mode. Hence, it is the mode in which important affective aspects of interest, perseverance, confidence, valuing, and the like are displayed. Since these factors are very important in the individual's willingness to pursue mathematics study, they are justifiably among the major aims in the new curriculum and must be a part of any assessment program.

5. Linked with affect and communication are the *social* variables. This is the mode in which much social functioning is based. Thus, we would expect to see some attempt to focus on an individual's capacity to work with others on mathematically related tasks.

It is clear that the ikonic mode can be used alone or in conjunction with other modes. It is also clear that it has been much neglected and deserves considerable attention in its own right in the mathematics classroom. Ability to use this mode is shown by a willingness to approach a problem with a relaxed and interested attitude similar to that of the preschool child's approach (Collis, 1988). There should not be a feeling that mathematics *belongs* to the concrete-symbolic mode and that a problem must be immediately translated into this form. This means that instruction must encourage an intuitive, relaxed approach and build up a feeling of confidence in adopting it. When designing items for this mode then, there are four obvious guidelines:

1. Sufficient background information (often in narrative form) must be supplied in a domain to which the student can relate that enables him or her to get the "picture" and to ignore any irrelevant information provided;
2. Care must be taken to ensure optimal performance by ensuring that students know what is expected and/or have available suitable models that indicate in general the kind of approach(es) expected;
3. The assessor must ensure that translation to the concrete-symbolic mode is obviously not a suitable first step; and
4. The closed item will rarely be a suitable format, but most open-ended item formats should be adaptable for use in this mode.

The concrete-symbolic mode has the following characteristics:

1. This is the mode in which *symbol systems* such as elementary mathematics are developed. As was explained earlier in this paper, there is logic and order in the system that allow for both independent and interdependent manipulation without breaking the essential direct link with the empirical world. In the context of both mathematics and this paper, this arrangement means that the reasoning and procedures fundamental to and typical of that domain are incorporated in this mode.
2. Mathematical *concepts* are the elements of thought for the concrete-symbolic mode. They are of a higher order of abstraction than the signifiers of the ikonic mode but are still directly related to the empirical world.
3. *Communication* is via propositional statements using the rules and concepts of the system.

It is clear that a large part of school mathematics instruction has always been concerned with teaching the concepts and procedures of mathematics in this mode. It is also clear that in problem solving, this mode, although it can be used alone, is most often required in conjunction with other modes. This last fact was not always considered in the traditional curriculum but is an essential element in the thrust of the new curriculum. The two facts together highlight some instructional requirements that are relevant to our purposes here.

First, it points to the need for teaching to take advantage of the student's abilities in *other* modes while focusing the instruction in the mode of immediate concern (Collis & Biggs, in press). Second, practice in translating the information given in the problem into a suitable concrete-symbolic format is a skill that is too often presumed to exist or is learned incidentally by the student when, in fact, it requires instructional attention. Finally, and related to the second, specific instruction needs to be given in recognizing classes of mathematical situations that will be amenable to well-recognized and well-known standard mathematical solutions.

In designing items to test in this mode, some general guidelines can be set down:

1. Unless selecting the mode to work in is part of the test, the information given should clearly indicate that the problem belongs to the concrete-symbolic mode;
2. To ensure optimal performance, students should be informed of what is expected in their response;
3. Sufficient and necessary information must be given to enable the students to pick the category of problem involved, especially if it is one in which irrelevant information is included; and
4. Both open and closed items are suitable for testing in this mode; each has its strengths for particular purposes and should be used alone or in conjunction as required.

To conclude this section, it is relevant to note one caveat. The aims of this new curriculum seem to emphasize multimodal functioning as defined earlier, but a close reading of summaries of some of the assessment recommendations (e.g., the *Standards*) seems to show a bias towards concrete-symbolic functioning. This is reasonable in one respect since the content area under consideration is *mathematics*, not *general* reasoning/problem solving. However, too much emphasis on the concrete-symbolic mode in assessment will tend to put us back where we were with the traditional curriculum. On the other hand, it is equally important to keep in mind that *mathematics* is what we have in mind and assessment must clearly reflect this. Balancing and integrating these competing demands will not be the least of the assessors' problems.

SUMMARY AND CONCLUSION

What has the analysis set out in the last two sections to offer the practitioner who is faced with the task of evaluating students' achievement in the light of the new curriculum aims? Basically, it has attempted to lay down a foundation in cognitive theory from which to view the new developments as they affect learning and its evaluation in mathematics. In particular, it highlighted the isomorphism between different kinds of cognitive functioning and different approaches to solving mathematics problems. It is asserted that these two factors are the key to developing both teaching strategies and assessment techniques. The first provides a research-based theoretical foundation to use as a guide and the second points the way to specific strategies which should be effective in practice. Let us examine these thoughts in relation to assessment.

There are two major aspects to be considered: devising suitable items and coding responses to those items. In neither case do the traditional models offer much help. In fact, the traditional way of doing things might well be counterproductive. For example, the traditional examination was developed by, at most, a few experts and kept secret from instructors and students alike. This procedure is diametrically opposed to the major aims of the new curriculum which tries to optimize performance, to test what students know, to encourage students' participation in their own learning, to test largely for instructional purposes, and so on. What then are the major steps that would seem to be necessary for devising items that take into account both the new aims and the theoretical position taken in this paper?

First, it would seem that all who have a stake in the learning process should have some part in devising ways of assessing the outcomes. Because they have maturity in the subject matter, in knowledge of the cognitive variables involved, in the aims of the program, and in program content and sequence, the instructors should play the major role. They should form a panel that draws up the first draft of items, for example, and seek feedback from other participants before finalizing the item, taking the feedback into account.

In organizing their first draft of an item, the panel might well begin by deciding what features they wish to include and at what level. This could be done by means of a table with the aims on one axis and the level of functioning on the other, as in Table 7-1.

Having deciding on the required pattern for the item(s), the panel would then devise or find item(s) that seemed to conform to the guidelines established. Alternatively, the panel could begin with a set of items and analyze them according to the suggested format, and then select for use those items that fit the criteria they had in mind at the time. Obviously, some items would need minor adjustments to ensure that they clearly served their intended purpose.

At this point in the process, arrangements of the items or parts of the items should be tried out, by individual interview, with a small sample of the students for whom they are intended. This would be expected to provide feedback to the panel so that the items can be adjusted to take account of the way in which the items are interpreted by the students. Sometimes students interpret a question as belonging to the ikonic mode when the instructor intends a concrete-symbolic interpretation; at other times, the wording of the

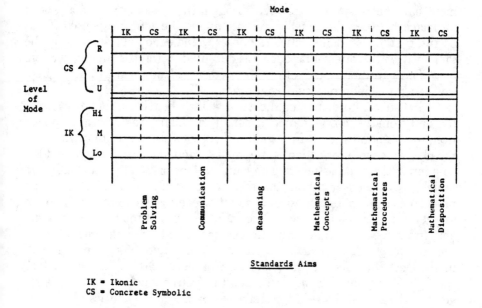

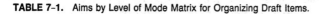

IK = Ikonic
CS = Concrete Symbolic

TABLE 7-1. Aims by Level of Mode Matrix for Organizing Draft Items.

item or the question, although perfectly clear and obvious to the assessors, may present unintended complexity to the students.

In summary, then, the task of designing items to test the aims of the new curriculum is one that (1) requires the cooperative effort of all participants, and (2) involves a detailed task analysis at several stages of item development. The former includes feedback from those due to take the final version of the test and the latter must be clearly tied to both the aims and the kinds and levels of functioning detailed earlier.

The next stage is concerned with assessing the students' responses for evaluation purposes. In the new content, this is basically for instructional purposes and, although concentrated on what the students know, the process should show where they are with what can reasonably be expected to be known. This would imply the availability of sample responses against which students' responses can be judged. These are probably best obtained by a quasi-cooperative process. The original panel, with the benefit of the detailed task analyses carried out earlier, could prepare an outline of their expectations and these can be filled out and/or adjusted in the light of a sample of the actual student responses made during the assessment. The sample responses would be accompanied by commentary that would specify the manner in which the response did or did not satisfy the category criteria determined in relation to the original task analysis. If the earlier steps of the item development have been carefully followed through, there should not be a serious mismatch between the panel's expectations and the actual responses. If this occurs, then the students' actual responses would need to be analyzed in the same way as the original task analysis and used as the basis for evaluation.

Three further aspects of testing need consideration at this point: item statistics, tabulation of results, and scoring.

Statistical information on the items will still be relevant but, because of the shift from the norm-referencing paradigm, will have a different emphasis from the traditional form. Instead of difficulty levels, age/grade norms, and the like, we need information on the mode(s) and aims being tested and the content/background assumed. The basic notions of validity, reliability, and usability will need attention, the first being largely taken care of by the procedures used in item construction. The second will require correlation of categories rather than of scores. The third, because of the techniques available (from restricted-time tests through individual or group interviews to semester-long individual or group projects), will require more attention than in the past. In selecting or devising items, instructors will have to look carefully at the aim(s) being tested and the instructional information being generated—a need that must be reflected by the item statistics.

Because each child learns mathematics individually and our aim is to increase personal mathematical power as defined in the *Standards*, the results need to be recorded to show each child's personal performance. Class averages and percentile rankings are largely irrelevant to this exercise. A well-organized testing program will not only give details of the child's mode and level of functioning in a particular item but, over several items, will give a general picture of the typical performance with mathematical material and act as a measure of the child's current level of mathematical power. The individual item results could be recorded on a grid similar to the task analysis grid or in a histogram format with the objectives forming the categories on the horizontal axis and the modal levels being indicated vertically. One way of deriving the general summary of mathematical power would be to take the "line of best fit" between the levels shown in the various categories in the histograms over all the items in the test.

This brings us to the problem of assigning numbers or grades to students' results on items and tests. This procedure has a long tradition behind it but was clearly much more appropriate under an earlier paradigm. Number scores have been used basically to reflect variability between students, although they were also intended much of the time to put some absolute value on the person's performance. It is doubtful if the procedures were ever valid in educational measurement since they assumed unidimensionality of the scale upon which they were based—an assumption unlikely to be met in most cases. The technique described here is clearly multidimensional and thus any assignment of a number on the basis of one dimension being involved is invalid and, moreover, quite without meaning. It is feasible that by using multidimensional scaling techniques, valid and meaningful numbers could be obtained; however, there would need to be considerable research into possible techniques before a decision to use such a method was made. And there is no intention to speculate on this area here.

APPENDIX:
EXAMPLES OF ITEM ANALYSIS

In analyzing an item, the basic modes that we need to consider are the ikonic and the concrete-symbolic. In the case of the latter, we need to place it at the level concerned; in the former case, in the absence of research, we need to consider whether there is a high, low, or medium involvement. Levels in the concrete-symbolic mode must be interpreted in terms appropriate to each specific item. The general model applicable to the concrete-symbolic mode is shown in Figure 7-2 in the body of the text. Let us recall the basic characteristics:

> *Unistructural:* one element or process characteristic of the concrete-symbolic mode is present and thus the student engages in the exercise in a mathematically meaningful way.
>
> *Multistructural:* several elements are involved; appropriate terms and processes are used but in a nonintegrated sequence.
>
> *Relational:* all the elements are used with appropriate processes; the whole approach is integrated into a well-balanced response which, however, does not go outside the given context to look at other possibilities.

For each item, a table, as shown and described in the text (p. 113), should be drawn up to facilitate consideration of the contribution of each mode to the aims already established. As can be seen, each table consists of two parts: the upper cells indicate the level in the concrete-symbolic mode while the lower cells show the use made of the ikonic mode. The entry in each cell is considered only in relation to the item and independently of the other cells. When the entries have been made, one can look at both the overall emphasis in the item/response as well as at the pairs of cells within the one aim. In addition, the two blocks of cells making up the table can be examined to investigate the interaction between the two modes in the item being considered. The technique described can be generalized to incorporate other modes of functioning (i.e., sensorimotor or formal) when necessary, but, in line with our stated intention in this paper, we are confining our attention to the concrete-symbolic and ikonic modes. The examples we have selected to illustrate our suggestion are taken from responses to items given by the California State Department of Education (1989) since their project has one of the few sets of data available on constructed-response items. This is not an ideal situation, as items were not constructed according to the

---

Item analyses in this Appendix are from the author's 1989 report for the California State Department of Education entitled *A Question of Thinking: A First Look at Students' Performance on Open-ended Questions in Mathematics.* Used by permission.

models described, but it will suffice to illustrate the points being made. This situation, however, does give us the opportunity to compare/contrast the assessors' a priori expectations/assumptions with respect to the item with the students' actual responses.

Problem A
Imagine you are talking to a student in your class on the telephone and want the student to draw some figures. The other student cannot see the figures. Write a set of directions so that the other student can draw the figures exactly as shown below.

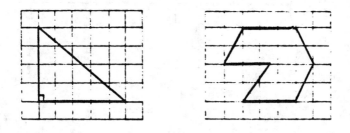

General Expectations
Ability to communicate mathematical ideas with clarity is an important compo-nent of mathematical power as emphasized in the California State Department of Education's *Mathematics Framework* for California Public Schools: Kinder-garten through Grade 12. Good communication, both verbal and written, indicates understanding. Understanding of a problem and ability to think are prerequisites to successful problem solving. Problem A assessed the skills of communicating about geometric shapes. It requires students to use effective terminology to describe the necessary features, in correct steps, to reproduce the given geometric shapes. Responses revealed how well students formulated and communicated mathematical ideas. No single solution or method was correct. An effective solution would result in the precise reproduction of the figures. The use of the word *exact* in the problem implied that the student's written directions would preserve the scale and orientation of the figures. It was also hoped that the instructions would be concise, mathematically elegant, and easy to follow. (California State Department of Education, 1989, p. 7)

Let us take these statements as the committee's task analysis and examine them in terms of the proposed structure.

SUMMARY OF EXPECTATIONS IN RELATION TO THE OBJECTIVES OF THE NCTM *STANDARDS*

- Problem solving: Not applicable.
- Communication: Mathematical description in a series of discrete steps marks a multistructural concrete-symbolic expectation; a medium level of visualization would be required to "picture" the effect of asking someone to *draw* a horizontal/vertical line, or the like.
- Reasoning: Not applicable.

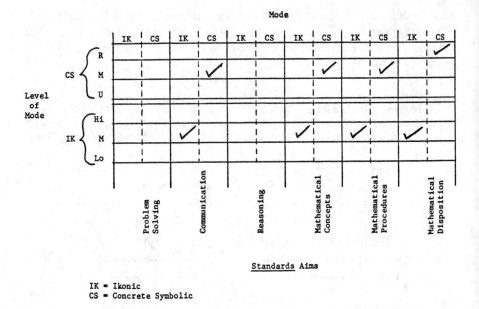

IK = Ikonic
CS = Concrete Symbolic

Task Analysis Table for Problem A (Assessors)

- Mathematical concepts: Understanding of terminology such as vertical, horizontal, and right triangle is at the multistructural concrete-symbolic level and, again, a medium degree of visualization is required to "picture" the result of the instruction at the other end of the telephone line.
- Mathematical procedures: Drawing to preserve features of orientation and scale is at a multistructural concrete-symbolic level and, as before, a medium level of visualization is required to "picture" the result of the instruction.
- Mathematical disposition: Concern for conciseness and elegance is at least relational in the concrete-symbolic mode but seems a little out of place in an exercise of this degree of difficulty. However, the assessors indicate that they were hoping for an integrated overview, possibly followed by an editing of the response, hence a relational-level expectation. From the point of view of the ikonic mode, the most that could be expected was a feeling of satisfaction that the task was correctly carried out; hence, a medium level engagement could be expected in this mode.

The assessors have set an exercise that is firmly in the concrete-symbolic mode. Moreover, the nature of the question requires only a multistructural-level response to be answered adequately. However, there are two distracting elements that would probably cause problems for the average student.

First, the telephone conversation image sets the scene for oral communication (ikonic mode) rather than propositional communication (concrete-symbolic mode). This could lead some students to ignore the mathematical concepts involved and to put forward an ikonic description more appropriate for an art class.

Second, the use of the term *exactly* is vague and assumes that the student will have at least a relational-level view of what the assessor might mean. Many students would not see the point and would ignore it, others would be confused by it, and only the very best would be likely to interpret it as the assessors intended. It would appear that the assessors might have been trying to convert a basically multistructural-level question to a higher level; their concern for conciseness and elegance lends credence to this view as the latter qualities are not usually associated with multistructural responses. This method of almost surreptitiously upping the level of response required seems directly counter to the spirit of the new curriculum.

SUMMARY OF SOME STUDENT RESPONSES TO PROBLEM A

① THE FIGURE IS A RIGHT TRIANGLE WITH THE 90° ANGLE ON THE BOTTOM LEFT-HAND SIDE

② THE VERTICAL LEG IS 4 UNITS HIGH AND THE HORIZONTAL LEG IS 5 UNITS LONG

③ CONNECT THE TWO LEGS WITH THE HYPOTENUSE, WHICH IS $\sqrt{4}$ UNITS LONG

Student 1
(California State Department of Education, 1989, p. 8)

The engagement of the ikonic mode would appear to be at least at the medium level although the student relies mainly on his knowledge of the concrete-symbolic system involved. For example, the first statement gives an overall "picture" of the completed figure by reference to a "right triangle" and specifying the position of the 90° angle. In the concrete-symbolic mode, the student has performed up to the multistructural criteria set by the assessors.

Place your pencil on the corner intersection of two squares. Draw a straight horizontal line to the right from that point at the length of five squares. Place your pencil at the first point described. Draw a vertical line up from the point at the length of four squares. From there draw a diagonal line down to the end of the first completed line to form a triangle.

Student 2
(California State Department of Education, 1989, p. 9)

This student has concentrated the description in the ikonic mode, visualizing the figure and concentrating on getting the partner to reproduce the visualization. The concrete-symbolic mode is represented by the use of appropriate terms but is used basically as a supplement. Thus, the communication category would be at least medium in the ikonic mode, at most unistructural in the concrete-symbolic mode; the other categories are arguably at the levels expected by the assessors.

Ðraw a parrallel line
On bottom make line straight aceross
about 3" inches then connect the end
of bottom with top of parallel line make
small square at corner of rectangle

Draw straight flat line with
two slanted lines on the side
on right one come down the
same opposite side, and on left
side make 2 inches inside cut
than draw away from it, the
now connect both to corners

Student 3
(California State Department of Education, 1989, p. 10)

These responses (both figures) seem to show that the student has tried to carry out the task almost entirely in the ikonic mode. It shows that he/she has a reasonable visualization of the figures but very little knowledge of the concrete-symbolic system. This information is valuable for the teacher since it shows where remediation activities need to be concentrated.

Problem C
James knows that half of the students from his school are accepted at the public university nearby. Also, half are accepted at the local private college. James thinks that this adds up to 100%, so he will surely be accepted at one or the other institution. Explain why James may be wrong. If possible, use a diagram in your explanation.

General Expectations
An important aspect of mathematical power is the need to use logic and diagrams to make sense of a situation and to communicate this reasoning. Diagrams represent an effective analytical and communications tool. Problem C assesses the ability to detect erroneous reasoning and requires a clear and mathematically correct explanation of the faulty reasoning. Specifically, the

problem demands a recognition that acceptances from the different institutions are not mutually exclusive. The students' responses should focus on the faulty reasoning involving James's assumption of nonoverlapping sets. A variety of diagrams or explanations could be used to help clarify the situation; no particular one was preferred. (California State Department of Education, 1989, p. 21)

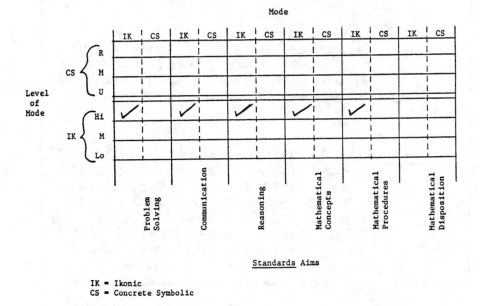

IK = Ikonic
CS = Concrete Symbolic

Task Analysis Table for Problem C

SUMMARY OF EXPECTATIONS IN RELATION TO THE OBJECTIVES OF THE NCTM *STANDARDS*

- Problem solving: The assessors set this as a nonroutine problem and their expectations indicate an emphasis on the ikonic mode rather than on the concrete-symbolic mode.
- Communication: Students' attention is focused on diagrams as the prime means of explanation and communication.
- Reasoning: The reasoning involves visualization, imaging, and use of knowledge gained from experience rather than anything specifically mathematical.
- Mathematical concepts: The assessors are not expecting the use of any specific concrete-symbolic mathematical concepts; the nonroutine nature of the problem relies rather on the general notion of nonexclusiveness of the selection process rather than a "formal" knowledge of disjoint and intersecting sets.
- Mathematical procedures: The implicit expectation in using diagrams or explanations to clarify the situation seems to be that the diagrams would incorporate a visual representation of the intersecting sets involved.
- Mathematical disposition: Not applicable.

**SUMMARY OF SOME STUDENT RESPONSES
TO PROBLEM C**

Student 1
(California State Department of Education, 1989, p. 23)

This student has a clear overall picture of the problem and has been able to focus his/her image on the essential mathematical aspects without any attempt to translate into the concrete-symbolic mode. He/she has performed up to the high level of the ikonic mode expected by the assessors. The fact that the figures have been drawn carrying or not carrying book(s) contributes both to the communication and mathematical procedures aims, while the essential set-related mathematical concepts are clearly in place. The mathematical reasoning aim in this ikonic context is well illustrated by the introduction of the set of people not going on to college or university. Finally, although the assessors had no expectations listed regarding mathematical disposition, this student has shown quite a high level of ikonic mode engagement in this area. The evidence is available both from the overall whimsical approach to the diagram and from the subtleties in the final character, "ain't be goin' to school" (not college or university), and facial expression.

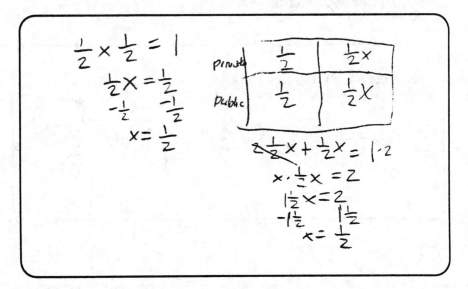

Student 2
(California State Department of Education, 1989, p. 26)

An attempt has been made to make an immediate translation into the concrete-symbolic mode. The meaningless doodling which follows certainly indicates that the student has no concrete-symbolic mathematical procedure available in this context to manipulate the symbols created by the translation, but it does give some indication of how the student (incorrectly) perceives the mathematical problem-solving process in general. For whatever reason, this student has not involved the ikonic mode at any point.

> Thats wRong because every one doesnt go to college I think it
>
> 15% doesnt go
> 4/5 That goes to ·local college
> 90 That goes to private college

Student 3
(California State Department of Education, 1989, p. 25)

This example shows a low level of ikonic-mode functioning combined with a low level (unistructural) of performance in the concrete-symbolic mode.

Problem E
The square shown below has sides of length 2 units. Connect the midpoints of the sides of the square, in order, to form an *interior* square. Repeat the same process to make squares within squares.
(a) Draw the first five *interior* squares.
(b) Write the sequence of numbers that represent the areas of the first five *interior* squares.
(c) What rule can be used to find the areas of the *n*th *interior* square?

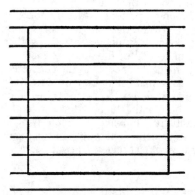

General Expectations
In Problem E, students had to follow directions to draw a figure showing the telescoping of five interior squares. Then they had to calculate the areas of the interior squares, organize the information so that any pattern present could be observed, and conjecture about a general rule that could govern the situation. Algebra II textbooks frequently include problems similar to this one that challenge students' creativity. (California State Department of Education, 1989, p. 36)

SUMMARY OF EXPECTATIONS IN RELATION TO
THE OBJECTIVES OF THE NCTM *STANDARDS*

This question has three parts that need to be considered separately. To conserve space and to provide an alternative to the tabulation suggested for the earlier items, each part will be analyzed in note form.

1. Part (a), the drawing of the first five *interior* squares. The assessors were expecting a concrete-symbolic relational level of understanding of mathematical concepts associated with the concrete-symbolic terms (square, midpoints of sides, interior squares) and a high level of ikonic functioning involved in visualizing the "telescoping" effect of following the directions. No other of the *Standards* aims seems to be of much import, as the completion of this part of the exercise appears to be dependent upon the correct interpretation of the terms and directions given.

2. Part (b), the sequence of numbers that represent the areas of the squares. The expectations here covered several of the *Standards* aims, with all but one in the concrete-symbolic mode: problem solving (how to go about the task effectively, e.g., find the length of each side in turn and calculate the area

of the square associated); reasoning (the detailed way of translating the problem-solving notion into practice, e.g., use Pythagorean theorem [or known ratio] to find side of first interior square, square the result for first area and record, halve side of first interior square, etc.) mathematical concepts (areas, hypotenuse/sides relationship, etc.); mathematical procedures (use of procedures: Pythagorean relationships, squaring, roots, surds, etc.)—all are at the top of the relational level of the concrete-symbolic mode. In addition, the reasoning involved quite a high level of the ikonic mode because it requires a high degree of imaging skill to keep track of the dimensions as one moves further into the interior of the figure.

3. Part (c), finding a pattern in the numbers recording the areas of the squares. In this part of the question, the assessors were expecting relational-level functioning, concrete-symbolic mode, together with high-level ikonic-mode functioning in several of the areas defined by the *Standards* aims. For example, the mathematical concepts in the concrete-symbolic mode were concerned with the mathematical notion of series/sequences while the same variable in the ikonic mode was represented by the need to visualize patterns. Problem solving required the highest level in both modes, while reasoning required only a multistructural level, concrete-symbolic mode, but a high level of ikonic-mode involvement. The only other aim represented, mathematical procedures, necessitated relational-level concrete-symbolic involvement but no ikonic-mode input.

Before looking at some student responses, a comment on the item in the context of this paper seems necessary. As an item designed for the new curriculum, it has two serious weaknesses. First, its sequential arrangement makes success in the later parts very much dependent upon success in the earlier parts. A successful, but cumbersome, approach in an earlier part adds unnecessarily to a student's cognitive load as he/she moves into a later part. An unsuccessful attempt at an earlier part virtually precludes success in later parts. Second, the assessors' notion of "conjecturing about a general rule" suggests that they had an aspect of the formal mode in mind (hypothesizing and testing) when setting what seems originally to have been intended as a concrete-symbolic mode question. This inadvertent mixing of modes makes it difficult for both student and teacher to determine the expectations in relation to the aims.

**SUMMARY OF SOME STUDENT RESPONSES
TO PROBLEM E**

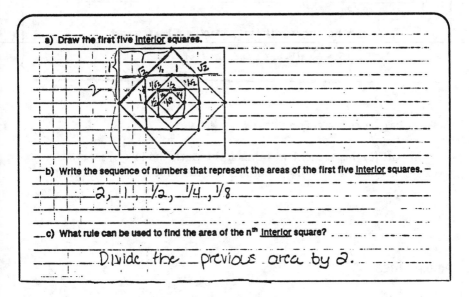

Student 1
(California State Department of Education, 1989, p. 37)

If we judge by the small amount of work shown, the dimensions on the squares, this student has performed as suggested in the analysis of the assessors' expectations set out above.

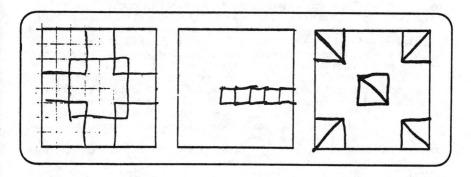

Students 2–4
(California State Department of Education, 1989, p. 38)

These students failed to reach the required level in either the concrete-symbolic mode (relational) or the ikonic mode (high).

Student 5
(California State Department of Education, 1989, p. 41)

In part (c) this student was unable to reach the levels required in the modes concerned for finding a pattern in the numbers already obtained.

REFERENCES

ALEXANDER, L., & JAMES, H.T. (1987) *The nation's report card*. Cambridge, MA: National Academy of Education.

BIGGS, J.B., & COLLIS, K.F. (in press). Developmental learning and the quality of intelligent behavior. In H. Rowe (Ed.), *Intelligence: Reconceptualization and measurement*. Melbourne: ACER.

BIGGS, J.B., & COLLIS, K.F. (1982). *Evaluating the quality of learning: The SOLO taxonomy*. New York: Academic Press.

BINET, A., & SIMON, T. (1908). Le developpement de l'intelligence chez les enfants. *Année Psychologiqua, 14,* 1-94.

BRUNER, J.S. (1964). The course of cognitive growth. *American Psychologist, 19,* 1-15.

CALIFORNIA STATE DEPARTMENT OF EDUCATION (1989). *A question of thinking: A first look at students' performance on open-ended questions in mathematics*. Sacramento: Author.

CAMPBELL, P.F., & FEY, J.T. (1988). New goals for school mathematics. In R.S. Brandt (Ed.), *Content of the curriculum; 1988 ASCD yearbook* (pp. 53-74). Alexandria, VA: Association for Supervision and Curriculum Development.

CARPENTER, T.P., & MOSER, J.M. (1982). The development of addition and subtraction problem-solving skills. In T.P. Carpenter, J.M. Moser, & T.A. Romberg (Eds.), *Addition and subtraction: A cognitive perspective* (pp. 9-24). Hillsdale, NJ: Lawrence Erlbaum Associates.

CARPENTER, T.P., & MOSER, J.M. (1983). The acquisition of addition and subtraction concepts. In R. Lesh & M. Landau (Eds.), *The acquisition of mathematical concepts and processes* (pp. 7-44). New York: Academic Press.

CARPENTER, T.P., & MOSER, J.M. (1984). The acquisition of addition and subtraction concepts in grades one through three. *Journal for Research in Mathematics Education, 15,* 179-202.

CARRAHER, T.N. (1989). Numeracy without schooling. In *Actes de la 13eme Conference Internationale I*. Paris, France: PME.

CARRAHER, T.N. (1988). *Adult mathematical skills: The contribution of schooling*. Paper presented at the annual meeting of AERA, New Orleans, April 1988.

CARRAHER, T.N., CARRAHER, D.W., & SCHLIEMANN, A.D. (1985). Mathematics in the street and in schools. *British Journal of Developmental Psychology, 3,* 21-29.

CASE, R. (1985). *Cognitive development*. New York: Academic Press.

CHI, M.T.H., GLASER, R., & REES, E. (1982). Expertise in problem solving. In R. Sternberg (Eds.), *Advances in the psychology of human intelligence, Vol. 1.* Hillsdale, NJ: Lawrence Erlbaum Associates.
CHIPMAN, S., SEGAL, J., & GLASER, R. (EDS.). (1984). *Thinking and learning skills.* Hillsdale, NJ: Lawrence Erlbaum Associates.
COLLIS, K.F. (1988). The "add up" or "take away" syndrome. In J. Pegg (Ed.), *Mathematical interfaces, Proceedings of the 12th Biennial Conference of AAMT.* Newcastle, UK.
COLLIS, K.F. (1975). *A study of concrete and formal operations in school mathematics: A Piagetian viewpoint.* Melbourne: ACER.
COLLIS, K.F., & BIGGS, J.B. (in press). Developmental determinants of qualitative aspects of school learning. In G.T. Evans (Eds), *Learning and teaching cognitive skills.* Melbourne: ACER.
COLLIS, K.F., & BIGGS, J.B. (1983). Matriculation, degree requirements, and cognitive demands in universities and CAEs. *Australian Journal of Education, 27,* 41–51.
COMMONS, M.C., RICHARDS, F.A., & KUHN, D. (1982). Systematic and metasystematic reasoning: A case for levels of reasoning beyond Piaget's stage of formal operations. *Child Development, 53,* 1058–1069.
DECORTE, E., & VERSCHAFFEL, L. (1987). The effect of semantic structure on first graders' strategies for solving addition and subtraction word problems. *Journal for Research in Mathematics Education, 18,* 363–381.
DELANGE, J. (1987). *Mathematics insight and meaning.* Utrecht: OW & OC.
DEMETRIOU, A., & EFKLIDES, A. (1985). Structure and sequence of formal and postformal thought: General patterns and individual differences. *Child Development, 56,* 1062–1091.
DEMETRIOU, A., & EFKLIDES, A. (in press). Experiential structuralism and neo-Piagetian theories: Towards an integrated model. *International Journal of Psychology.*
DONALDSON, M. (1978). *Children's minds.* Glasgow: Fontana/Collins.
EGAN, K. (1984). *Educational development.* Oxford: Oxford University Press.
FISCHER, K.W. (1980). A theory of cognitive development: The control and construction of hierarchies of skills. *Psychological Review, 57,* 477–531.
FISCHER, K.W., & KENNY, S.L. (1986). Environmental conditions for discontinuities in the development of abstractions. In R.S. Mines & K.S. Sitchener (Eds.), *Adult cognitive development: Methods and models.* New York: Praeger.
FISCHER, K.W., & KNIGHT, C.C. (in press). Cognitive development in real children: Levels and variations. In B. Presseisen (Ed.), *The at-risk student and thinking: Perspectives from research.* Washington, DC: National Education Association.
FISCHER, K.W., & PIPP, S. (1984). Process of cognitive development: Optimal level and skill acquisition. In R. Sternberg (Ed.), *Mechanism of cognitive development.* New York: Freeman.
FISCHER, K.W., & SILVERN, L. (1985). Stages and individual differences in cognitive development. *Annual Review of Psychology, 36,* 613–648.
GARDNER, H. (1985). *Frames of mind.* London: Paladin.
GREENE, H.A., JORGENSON, A.N., & GERBERICH, J.R. (1953). *Measurement and evaluation in the elementary school* (2nd ed.). New York: Longmans, Greene and Co.
HADAMARD, J. (1954). *The psychology of invention in the mathematical field.* Princeton University Press.
HALFORD, G.S. (1982). *The development of thought.* Hillsdale, NJ: Lawrence Erlbaum Associates.
HOYLES, C. (1987). Personal communication. University of London.
MATHEMATICAL SCIENCES EDUCATION BOARD (1989). *Everybody counts: A report to the nation on the future of mathematics education.* Washington, DC: National Academy Press.
MONOUD, P. (1985). Similarities between developmental sequences at different age periods. In I. Levin (Ed.), *Stage and structure.* New York: Ablex.
MURNANE, R.J., & RAIZEN, S.A. (EDS.). (1988). *Improving indicators of the quality of science and mathematics education in grades K–12.* Washington, DC: National Academy Press.
NATIONAL COUNCIL OF TEACHERS OF MATHEMATICS (1989). *Curriculum and evaluation standards for school mathematics.* Reston, VA: Author.
OAKES, J. (1986). *Educational indicators: A guide for policy makers.* Santa Monica, CA: Center for Policy Research in Education, The RAND Corporation.

PETERSON, P.L., FENNEMA, E., & CARPENTER, T.P. (in press). Using knowledge of how students think about mathematics. *Educational Leadership*.

PIAGET, J. (1950). *The psychology of intelligence*. London: Routledge & Kegan Paul.

RESNICK, L.B. (1987). Learning in school and out. *Educational Researchers, 16*(9), 13–20.

ROMBERG, T.A. (1988). *Changes in school mathematics: Curricular changes, instructional changes, and indicators of change*. New Brunswick, NJ: Center for Policy Research in Education, Eagleton Institute of Politics, Rutgers, The State University of New Jersey.

ROMBERG, T.A., & COLLIS, K.F. (1987). *Learning to add and subtract*. Monograph number 2, Journal for Research in Mathematics Education, National Council of Teachers of Mathematics.

SCRIBNER, S. (1986). Thinking in action: Some characteristics of practical thought. In R.J. Sternberg & R.K. Wagner (Eds.), *Practical intelligence*. Cambridge University Press.

STERNBERG, R.J., & WAGNER, R.K. (Eds.). (1986). *Practical intelligence*. Cambridge University Press.

VERGNAUD, G. (1982). A classification of cognitive tasks and operations of thought involved in addition and subtraction problems. In T.P. Carpenter, J.M. Moser, & T.A. Romberg (Eds.), *Addition and subtraction: A cognitive perspective* (pp. 39–59). Hillsdale, NJ: Lawrence Erlbaum Associates.

WEBB, N.L. (1987). Another look at assessment: A reaction to chapters 17–20. In T.A. Romberg & D.M. Stewart (Eds.), *The monitoring of school mathematics: Background papers: Vol. 2. Implications from psychology; outcomes of instruction* (pp. 243–260). Madison, WI: Wisconsin Center for Education Research, School of Education, University of Wisconsin-Madison.

WEBB, N., & ROMBERG, T. (1989). *Implications of the NCTM Standards for mathematics assessment*. Madison, WI: National Center for Research in Mathematical Sciences Education.

EIGHT

COGNITIVE ASSESSMENT OF HISTORY FOR LARGE-SCALE TESTING

Eva L. Baker
Marie Freeman
Serena Clayton

In this chapter Eva L. Baker, Marie Freeman, and Serena Clayton discuss implications of cognitive theory for the assessment of student learning in the social sciences. They report some recent research conducted at the UCLA Center for the Study of Evaluation. These studies focus on the measurement of comprehension using student essays to measure relationships among the ideas presented in the history texts, and between those ideas and student knowledge and experience. They discuss procedures useful for measuring these relationships in classes taught in secondary schools.

INTRODUCTION

For at least a quarter of a century, educators and critics have raised conceptual and technical questions about standardized achievement tests (Strenio, 1981). And for the most part, the public and its policymakers have ignored these ululations and continued to believe in the accuracy and usefulness of these measures, dismissing technical concerns as abstrusely academic and teacher complaints, at minimum, as self-serving. However, recent reform efforts, stemming from *A Nation At Risk* (National Commission for Educational Excellence, 1983) and other dark reports of American educational quality, have directed renewed attention and investment in achievement outcomes. With the statement of national educational goals by the President in 1990 and the governors of the fifty states in 1989, and the President's promise to measure achievement in grades 4, 8, and 12, standardized achievement tests are about to become national educational policy. The consequences of error in test design and interpretation are inestimably higher than in the past, for such measures will exert dramatic control on the public school curriculum, on what tests are published, and on what is taught. Information from achievement measures must answer three questions: What is the quality of our students' achievement? How can achievement be improved? Why can't present tests do the job? For the purposes of accountability and instructional improvement, the vast majority of existing standardized achievement tests are wholly inadequate. They create the wrong expectations and incite inaccurate inferences in terms of policy action. They are inappropriate in at least three central ways: their underlying theory, their content, and their procedures. These assertions deserve at least brief elaboration.

The measurement assumptions of standardized tests rely on models based on theories of stable individual differences. These models posit a general construct such as mathematics ability or reading comprehension. Construct measurement has at least two requirements: (a) substantial variation among people on the target test in order to differentiate scores, that is, scores on the 78th or 64th percentile are intended to reflect different levels of performance; and (b) stability of measurement for individual performance for

The research reported herein was conducted with partial support from the U.S. Department of Education, Office of Educational Research and Improvement, pursuant to Grant No. G0086-003. However, the opinions expressed do not necessarily reflect the position or policy of this agency and no official endorsement by this agency should be inferred.

We wish to thank Tom Kerins, John Craig, and Carmen Chapman, of the Illinois State Board of Education; Bob Hill, of the Springfield Public Schools; Lynn Winters, of the Palos Verdes School District; and the many principals and English and history teachers who participated in or helped with this project. In addition, we would like to thank colleagues at UCLA who helped with various aspects of the study: Pam Aschbacher, Jamal Abedi, Joan Herman, Edys Quellmalz, Merl Wittrock, Simon Chang, Yujing Ni, Regie Stites, Kim Kyung-Sung, and Rebecca Frazier.

accurate prediction. When mapped against the requirements for assessing an individual's educational improvement or the impact of systemic educational reform, these instruments do not measure up. Reports from most standardized tests obscure the meaning of the test scores from the teacher, the student, and the public. We may know the relative position of individuals and school districts compared to other individuals or school districts, but we do not know what level of performance any given score describes. Further, even under the best conditions, educational reform has weak effects. So to detect change, progress toward national goals, for example, achievement measures must be created that are sensitive to minor, but real differences in performance. Tests should tell us who has *changed* in ability to perform particular tasks at described levels of expertise. Standardized achievement tests do not tell us what we should want to know.

The problem of interpreting these tests is amplified by the way their content is selected. A major problem is content sampling within a particular subject matter, such as history or mathematics. Most subject matter measures are commercially available and are intended to be sold to school districts and states. To be competitive, testing companies must attempt to include a sufficient number of topics with broad appeal in any subject matter. A common result, as predicted two decades ago (Popham & Husek, 1969), is a content-curriculum mismatch, where the overlap on test content and curriculum varies by district, school, or classroom. This phenomenon has been documented in many specific subject fields, for example, in mathematics by Floden and his colleagues (1980). In practical terms, a mismatch means that certain topics that are untreated in the curriculum of given classrooms and schools will be included on the test. On the other hand, even topics emphasized in teaching may only be superficially measured because of time constraints. Both types of errors result in misrepresenting students' actual achievement. One solution to this problem has been to encourage teachers to adapt their instruction to match test content (a process called "alignment"), a course of action that cedes enormous and inappropriate power to the developers of such tests.

A second, more global content issue is created by the pressure to test in a relatively limited number of subject matters. Such choices have been made as a matter of course to save money and time as well as to constrain the number of measures on which public accountability will be based. As a rule, districts and states commonly select an essential core of subject matter, often the areas of reading and computational skills in mathematics. Teachers and school policymakers adapt instructional time to focus on the goals to be measured. One consequence of this adaptation may be a reduction in time for untested subject fields: foreign language, the humanities, the arts, and the sciences. This reduction occurs logically to focus resources on the accountable aspects of the curriculum, but also because of the widespread, pernicious belief that students must learn the "basics" before they can profit from exposure to other subject matters and more complex intellectual processes. Particularly for poorly performing students, opportunities in a wide range of subject matter are foregone (Oakes, 1986). The result is obvious—an educational system with clearly constricted curricula, differentially skewed to limit the access of the already disadvantaged.

The constraints on administration and scoring of standardized tests also influence their impact on school learning. Tests have been developed with strict time boundaries, partly in an effort to reduce testing time, partly from historical, psychometric reasons as the result of their original purposes to differentiate among individuals. To obtain differentiated and reliable responses, it is better to limit test time and to expose students to many short items. More test items also mean more topics can be covered. Multiple-choice items are the most frequently preferred achievement testing format because they are time sensitive, permit responses to a relatively large set of items, have acceptable psychometric properties, and allow economical scoring approaches. How do these choices affect students? Multiple-choice formats exert undeniable control on school practice. The format frames how information is presented, learned, and retained. These tests assess learning in an artificial, decontextualized manner that is remote from how students learn or will apply knowledge in the future. These tests are likely to reduce student motivation to perform and are likely to inhibit transfer. Such formats also convey a false sense of objectivity and quantification of performance, and objectivity and quantification are high-priority attributes in our society.

If it is true that such tests measure content only partially represented in school instruction and use formats convenient for administration and scoring rather than for learning, the simple problem of showing "improvement" in achievement is difficult and daunting. If it is difficult to design programs whose effects are detected by accountability measures, educators have few acceptable options. They may persist in doing the best they can, but may continue to see public confidence erode when test scores do not respond to their efforts. They may react in ethically questionable or unacceptable ways, for instance, selecting tests that seem easiest rather than those that most accurately measure valid educational goals (Cannell, 1987; Linn, Graue, & Sanders, 1989), encouraging inappropriate practice of items on the test (Shepard, 1989; Popham, 1990), or even falsifying test results. Schools may respond by offering training programs to develop test-taking skills and may confuse, once again, ends and means. How do students, the nominal object of our concern, respond? From the broad evidence, it appears with less interest and focus at best, and with active subversion at worst. Thus, with the best intentions, policymakers, compliantly supported by the public, require standardized achievement measures as the principal indicator of educational effectiveness and continue to deform the system in serious ways. Even a partial acceptance of the analysis raises serious questions about the quality of inferences we are drawing from standardized tests.

New Choice Points

The expectation that accountability measures will directly and productively influence student achievement is wildly optimistic. Their imposition influences broad instructional choices: how much time is allocated to various subject matters, and what particular topics are covered. But to affect important student performances, measures must influence a far deeper and dynamic level of instructional decision making. They must provide guidance and be sensitive to differences not only in what topics should be included in the curriculum, but also to the dirty details of teaching and learning, the instructional processes that differentially affect performance. Unless measures are ultimately sensitive to significant instructional choices, their impact on school improvement will continue to be marginal, periodically stunning policy makers who use terms like "stall" to explain the dysfunction between their own accountability fantasies and the actual utility provided by test results for day-to-day instructional planning. One answer has been to search for alternatives to the existing tests that will provide help to improve instruction. Unfortunately, this strategy has resulted in the propagation of test functions with little linkage between them — for example, between diagnostic and accountability tests. We need measures that can provide information at the right level of detail to guide instruction but that will not divert large proportions of instructional time from learning tasks.

To meet the legitimate concerns for accountability and resulting instructional improvement, we require new approaches. It is time to break away from the inertia of present achievement testing practices, from the never-never-land thinking that we can make schools better only by trying harder. We need outcome measures that simultaneously avoid major deficits of standardized tests and provide trustworthy and useful achievement information. Critical attributes to be possessed by new cognitive approaches to testing are (a) they focus on important and teachable learning processes, (b) we can place confidence in their measurements, and (c) the cues they provide for instruction are appropriate.

Cognitively Sensitive Assessment

If we start with the notion that tests should measure significant learning in a way that supports desired performance, we are immediately led to a reversal of present practice. Instead of having tests constrain instruction, assessment procedures should be constructed to map directly on significant features of learning. Through close observation, skilled experts can tell whether learners are making progress on a wide range of intellectual tasks. Our problem is to transmute the critical aspects of that observational process into procedures suitable for use in large-scale assessment. We must shift our view from the measurement of broad constructs to the assessment of important and described classes of cognitive learning tasks — knowledge acquisition, deep understanding, and problem solving. These processes must be assessed as they are embedded in various tasks and content domains; however, our assessment strategies may attempt to capture attributes of performance that transfer across subject matter domains. In our CRESST project on assessing deep understanding of subject matter, we conducted research designed to transfer knowledge that developed in learning research and apply it to the problem of assessing the understanding of history. What will follow is a chronological description of the developmental history of our project, interpolated by discussions of the generalizable problems confronting developers of new approaches to assessment.

PROJECT GOALS AND PLANS: DEVELOPING NEW CRITERIA FOR SCORING WRITING IN HISTORY

Stimulated by articulate statements about the importance of knowledge of history by Hirsch, Kett, and Trefil (1987) and the dismal performance of American students on tests of historical knowledge (Ravitch & Finn, 1987), we decided to focus our attention on the measurement of history knowledge. We decided to attempt to assess a deeper understanding of history. We conceived of the problem for students as a comprehension task dependent on their ability to generate or construct meaning (Wittrock, 1974, 1990) from provided stimuli by activating students' prior knowledge. This approach contrasts with the conception of history knowledge as a single construct dependent on the accumulation of separate pieces of knowledge. Consequently, we broadened our approach from the usual multiple-choice format. Our research group had considerable experience in developing measures of writing skill (Baker, 1987; Quellmalz, Capell, & Chou, 1982). Our initial idea was to attempt to expand the content-quality scoring rubrics used to assess writing and to apply them to subject matter topics in the field of history. Extant content-quality scoring rubrics have treated content in one of two ways: as elaborated detail that contributes to a good essay in holistic scoring; or as important, unique material dependent on the particular topic presented the learner. This second conception guides approaches used in scoring Advanced Placement Tests in History (Vaughan, 1983) and in primary trait scoring in the National Assessment of Educational Progress (1990). In this topic-dependent approach, individuals with expertise in the assigned topical area meet and develop *post hoc* standards for the particular set of papers written. The benefit of this procedure is the development of scoring scales that are particularly appropriate for the topic assigned. However, that strength is at once a severe limitation: First, the level of specificity required to adapt scoring criteria to a particular topic inhibits their more general use for other, similar topics. Thus, every topic possesses a unique set of criteria. Combining such particularized assessments across a range of topics or over a number of years involves a complex scaling process, based on equating results for different topics. Among a number of flaws, a major consequence of scaling is the ambiguity of score meaning. A second limitation relates to the inferences for instruction that can be derived from such measures. If every topic requires a unique set of criteria, what guidance can be provided to the teacher to inform teaching processes to improve student performance? Only if the tasks and scoring criteria are made public—released by the test producers—can teachers guide students to meet such standards, and then only if the same tasks are used. The trick is to find the appropriate level of generality to describe criteria so they are simultaneously appropriate for the particular assessment topics and conceived in terms that can guide future instructional practice and assessment.

Goals

The goals of our assessment research in the measurement of deep understanding of history were (a) to develop valid formats for eliciting students' thoughtful explanations about history concepts, (b) to create and validate content-quality scoring criteria for students' responses, and (c) to explore these developments in the context of large-scale assessment settings. A longer-term interest is to communicate the test design characteristics so that they will be helpful to the design of effective teaching strategies.

Strategies

Target. In light of our technical expertise in writing assessment, our project focused attention on essay writing in history. We believed that the strong tradition for this type of task in history instruction would increase the chances, if successful, of widespread acceptance of new assessment strategies. We also determined from reviews of plans for state assessment activities that writing in social studies was planned for many of the more forward-looking state assessment enterprises (for instance, California, Connecticut, Illinois, and Michigan). Finally, we believed that the present approaches used in the scoring of content-focused writing were inappropriate both conceptually and practically for the dual purposes of measuring deep understanding in large-scale settings and providing inferences useful for instruction.

Plan. In order to verify the need for essay scoring systems to assess content quality, we first had to determine whether content specific scoring criteria for history already existed implicitly in the scoring behavior of history teachers. If so, we would identify these criteria, train others to use them, and validate their utility. If not, we would explore the literature to infer criteria that might be used. Even though our goal was to develop scoring approaches with reasonable generalizability across tasks to facilitate instructional improvement, we decided to limit our studies severely. We planned to focus on a grade level (eleventh grade) and on a single topic area in history, for we wished to be sure our findings were well grounded in a defined context. If we were encouraged by our results, we planned to test the generalizability of the approach: for other subject matter areas, for the age ranges of students for whom the approach was useful, and for sets of administration conditions. In sum, we anticipated the development of broadly useful assessment approaches as we conducted initial research in a restricted environment.

Our first problem was to identify specific content topics and strategy for data collection that would allow us to explore the issues of content-quality scoring criteria. One requirement was to assure that students had some previous exposure to the concepts we planned to assess so that they could respond to our tasks. We hoped to assign passages in commonly used textbooks for this purpose. To that end, we reviewed textbooks, literature on the teaching of history, and available curriculum guides to determine the topics and most desirable sections of secondary school textbooks appropriate for our experiments in measurement. Our review of textbooks led to unoriginal, but nonetheless depressing, results. For every topic we pursued, we discovered that secondary school texts presented relatively superficial treatments, without sufficient concepts and depth of supporting knowledge to allow the development of deep understanding. These views have been supported in the literature by Beck, McKeown, and Gromoll (1989), Sewall (1987), and FitzGerald (1979). We also consulted at length with the staff of the UCLA Center for the Study of Teaching and Learning in History, a collaborative enterprise of the National Endowment for the Humanities that brings together experts in history and curriculum.

Goal Redefinition

Because we were unable to identify suitable text segments for use in the assessment, we decided to incorporate the reading of a provided text as part of the assessment procedure itself. This decision transformed in a serious way our assessment focus. Rather than an exclusive focus on measuring the accumulation of information developed over a long period of instruction, we now attended to two major content issues: students' ability to read and integrate new information with previously learned knowledge, and students' ability to explain new ideas using their prior knowledge. This transformation placed our work squarely in line with cognitive views of language comprehension (Anderson, Spiro, & Anderson, 1978; Rumelhart, 1980; Brown, Bransford, Ferrara, & Campione, 1983; Kieras, 1985). However, we were still driven principally by our subject matter concerns, a fact that guided the formulation of criteria for the topic and text selection for assessment tasks displayed in Table 8–1.

Based on the application of these criteria, we decided that original speeches or essays composed by historical figures would meet criteria two, three, and five. For our initial set of studies, we selected the texts of the

TABLE 8-1. Criteria for the Selection of History Texts to Assess

1. Must be a regular and significant piece of the secondary school history curriculum in the United States.
2. Must depend on primary source material rather than summaries in textbook.
3. Must allow for multiple interpretations and inferences.
4. Must transcend immediate events and allow students to find relationships to other historical and contemporary events.
5. Must be brief enough to read within a class period.

Lincoln and Douglas debates on popular sovereignty and slavery, choices that met the remaining criteria as well.

Identification of Content-Quality Scoring Criteria: The First Pass

Our goal was to assemble valid criteria to assess understanding of history content. But essay writing consists of both content expertise and communication skills. We were well aware and troubled by the high intercorrelations in the literature between subscores on essays of expression skills and content knowledge (Baker & Quellmalz, 1980; Langer, 1984). Although it was obvious that highly verbal students would usually learn more about verbally based content areas, we were especially interested in discriminating performance between the ignorant facile writer with little subject matter understanding and the knowledgeable student with less developed writing skills. This desire corresponded to the common practice of high school teachers, who give both a "content" grade and a "form" grade (e.g., A−/B) on student essays. We wanted to focus on the elements that compose the content score.

A related concern was the impact of content knowledge (or lack thereof) on the raters' application of scores. We believed that knowledgeable people with experience in the subject matter would be needed to make the levels of distinction in which we were interested. Our first empirical study attempted to determine if the quality of content in essays—its accurateness, aptness, and structure—would be judged similarly by history teachers using implicit but common criteria for quality. We would contrast their ratings with those given by English teachers, specifically, teachers trained to score essays in terms of the quality of general writing skill or expression, such as organization, style, and purpose. The essays we collected for this study were provided by 85 eleventh-grade Advance Placement (AP) history students in a suburban high school. We chose AP students because they would be likely to write "scorable" papers, that is, produce a sufficient quantity of writing to be graded. The AP students also had been exposed to an instructional sequence on the pre-Civil War period approximately five months earlier, so they would possess some background knowledge of the topic.

The experimental procedures spanned two consecutive days. On the first day students were given a general multiple-choice examination in pre-Civil War history, a test that had been validated by six expert history teachers. Next, students completed a background questionnaire describing their grades in English and social studies, self-estimates in ability, interest in writing and social studies, and descriptions of teachers' instructional and assessment practices in history. On the second day, students were randomly assigned to read either the Lincoln or the Douglas debate text. After the students completed their reading, they were given an essay question in either a brief or an extended form that asked them to explain the author's main issues and why they were important. Students were allowed 50 minutes to read the text of the speech and to write their essay. The papers were independently scored by two groups of raters: the English teachers and the history teachers.

Procedures for English teacher raters.   One rater group was composed of four English instructors, all highly experienced in rating student essays according to holistic and analytic techniques. All had been trained to use the writing scoring scales developed at UCLA (Smith, 1978; Quellmalz, Smith, Winters, & Baker, 1980) and subsequently adapted for use in numerous state assessments, research studies, and the international comparisons of written composition performance (Baker, 1987). These scales included four major categories—general competence, essay organization, paragraph coherence, and support (meaning detail)—as well as scales for grammar and mechanics. We also were interested in the thought processes that raters used and their initial levels of stringency. Thus, we asked raters prior to their training to read three sample papers privately, to rate them on a five-point scale, and to comment on their decisions and impressions; comments were tape-recorded. Raters also were asked to identify criteria for a good paper. The training was conducted using procedures described by Quellmalz (1986) with model papers and illustrations of score points. The raters were told explicitly to focus on issues of presentation and rhetorical effectiveness rather than content-specific issues, such as content accuracy and depth of explanation. Nonetheless, during the training the raters insisted on modifying the scoring system: They decided to include as part the general competence subscore some index of the student's attention to the specific writing task. All raters independently scored each of the 85 papers.

Procedures for the history teachers.   Independently, and with no knowledge of the English teacher group or their resulting scores, a group of five history specialists was assembled to rate the same set of essays. Two were high school Advanced Placement teachers (from a school different than the data collection site) and three raters were advanced graduate students in history. Like the English teachers, all history raters were asked to assess three essays and to think aloud into the tape recorder as they completed this rating task. Their actual rating instructions differed dramatically from those given to the English teachers: No preexisting scoring scale was used, and no extensive training was conducted to determine if the history group shared implicit criteria. Each rater was told to give each paper two scores. The first score was to reflect how well the essay demonstrated serious understanding of the debate text read by the student. The second score was to provide an estimate of the essay's general quality, taking into account issues other than the essay's content. These scores conformed to the content-form scoring mentioned above. We also asked the history group to select the ten best and ten worst essays, so that we could infer from their choices the operational criteria they used to make their judgments. Each history teacher independently rated each of the 85 papers, giving each a content-quality and an overall quality score. Following the rating session, all teachers discussed in a group the attributes that distinguished the highest- from the lowest-rated papers.

Findings and Interpretations

Detailed data analyses were conducted; only the highlights will be reported here. No significant differences on student performance were found for text passage (Lincoln or Douglas) or question type (brief or extended), in the ratings of either group. Our findings verified the inappropriateness of the existing UCLA scoring scales for the content-focused task we used. Alpha coefficients among raters ranged from a low of 0.52 for mechanics to a high of 0.75 for general competence (the one score where raters took into account the task content). This finding reinforced the need for the development of a content-quality scoring rubric. For the history raters, the alpha coefficient on general quality was 0.69 and on content quality was 0.75. The generalizability ratings for English raters (4 raters by 4 subscales) was 0.65 and for history raters (5 raters by 2 subscores) was 0.73. An interesting finding was that the percentage of exact agreement for scores given in the history group to content quality was only 33%, suggesting that no clear set of implicit criteria was operating among the history specialists. In addition, a t test was computed between average scores given by the history teachers and the history graduate students; significantly higher scores were assigned by the secondary school history teachers. The correlation between general competence scores assigned by English teachers and history content quality scores on the same papers was 0.80, similar to the relationship between general competence assigned by the English group and the general quality score assigned by the history group (0.82). Such data suggested that English and history teachers were looking at papers in fundamentally similar ways.

Unfortunately, the expert knowledge possessed by history teachers did not seem to differentiate their judgment of student essays. But some aspect

TABLE 8-2. History Specialists' Generation of Criteria

Established the historical context

Presented a sound thesis early in the paper

Detail contributed to thesis was correct and was not simply opinion

Avoided absolute judgments

Presented multiple points of view

Avoided interpreting the past in terms of present conditions

of special knowledge was operating, however faint. A low but significant correlation was obtained between the content-quality scores of the history teachers and the total multiple-choice score ($r = 0.32$, $p < 0.05$). Leads for the development of content-quality scoring criteria had to come from other sources. We then reviewed the history raters' think-aloud ratings and their post-rating discussions of the ten best and worst papers. The historians agreed that the best papers had the qualities listed in Table 8-2.

Scoring Criteria: Pass Two

In an effort to explore the utility of these criteria, a comprehensive and detailed scoring rubric was constructed based on these categories. The 12-category scoring scheme comprised the elements listed in Table 8-3; these elements were to be used as scoring dimensions for the papers.

Detailed descriptions for each of five scale points for every category were prepared. Based on a brief tryout with raters and reviews by experts, however, we deemed that this comprehensive set of categories was too ambitious. A review of literature on characteristics of expert knowledge (see

TABLE 8-3. Scoring Criteria Inferred from Ratings of History Papers

Identification of the historical problem/central concept

Depth of elaboration

Breadth of elaboration

Flexibility

Fluency/detail

Evidence of an analytical problem

Goal orientation

Logical structure

Evidence of historical analysis

Autocriticism

Presentation

Style

Voss, 1978) suggested how we could pare the set down to five categories thought to represent critical attributes of historical thinking: historical context, depth of elaboration, breadth of elaboration, evidence, and historical analysis. In addition, we added two categories related to expression, rhetorical structure and mechanics, as well as an overall quality rating, general impression. New scale-point descriptions were generated for each of the eight categories, and model papers were assembled to illustrate particular attributes for training purposes. Four history raters (three AP history teachers and one history graduate student) were trained in the use of the new system. They spent two days rating the same set of 85 eleventh-grade papers used in the first study. Raters were observed as they scored papers and were queried about their satisfaction with the rating scales and training procedures. Raters had been given the scoring rubric in two forms: (1) an extended, multipaged form with detailed explanations about each score point for use in training, and (2) an outline of the dimensions. It was expected that after the initial training period the raters would use the outline form. However, they chose to continue to refer to the extended form, more rigidly adhering to the rubric than we expected. Raters reported that they could differentiate among categories and that they could also distinguish among criteria for score points (1–5) within each category. Raters were highly satisfied with the scoring categories and claimed to use similar criteria to score papers produced in their own classrooms.

Data from the second round of scoring were then analyzed. Unfortunately, the findings from these ratings did not significantly advance our research goal. Percentage of exact agreement among raters nudged up to about 35%, but alpha coefficients for rater agreement dropped to around 0.45. Most disappointing were relatively high intercorrelations (in the 0.80 range) among rating categories. These strong relationships were confirmed by a factor analysis that produced only two factors, one factor consisting solely of the mechanics rating and the other loading all other categories. These disappointing results forced us to regroup intellectually once again. Fortunately, we were able to compare the results from the first set of ratings by the five history teachers with this set of scores, since the identical student papers were read by both groups of history specialists. The categories in our revised rating scale that mostly highly correlated with the overall content-quality rating from the first experiment were historical context, breadth of elaboration, and depth of elaboration; these categories were set aside for future exploration.

We so far had investigated the existence of common implicit criteria for content-quality ratings, had analyzed the think-aloud protocols of raters, and had noted criteria used in identifying successful student papers. We then had created a comprehensive list of content-relevant elements, had reduced them to a smaller set of categories for feasibility purposes, and had trained a satisfied group of raters. Yet, we had not seemingly made much progress toward our goal. At this point we realized that our entire process had been guided in large measure by what history specialists *said* they valued and usually focused on when they graded papers. It became obvious that such descriptions might reasonably be influenced by the raters' desires to appear to be comprehensive and thoughtful—in other words, by the social desirability of their answers.

Scoring Criteria: Pass Three

A new strategy for developing scoring criteria was employed, using the model derived from expert-novice comparisons (see Chi & Glaser, 1980, for an illustration). Rather than focus on what experts *said* they did, we were going to study their *actual performance* on tasks identical to those provided the students. Three expert historians who were advanced graduate students in history, three secondary school history teachers, and three Advanced Placement students were asked to write answers to the same essay question used in the study above and to think aloud to permit us to assess their processes. The analyses of the essays produced by this process as well as our analyses of the think-aloud transcripts resulted in some clear direction for us in the area of criteria generation: Our analyses showed that all experts and some teachers used the elements in Table 8-4 to construct their essays.

In contrast, very bright but relatively inexperienced students and some teachers leaned heavily on the text in two ways. First, they often simply paraphrased or even restated the text in their answer. Second, they tried to cover all elements discussed in the text and were unable to distinguish between more- and less-important details. As a result of this analysis, a scoring scheme was developed that included all of the elements in Table 8-4, augmented by an overall general impression score. We were ready for new data collection.

Rethinking Our Task

The first major redirection of this project occurred because of the paucity of quality textbooks and resulted in turning this assessment research toward the dual goals of measuring understanding and knowledge acquisition in the context of a particular subject matter corpus. The expert-novice

TABLE 8-4. Elements Used by All Experts and Some Teachers in Essay Construction

A strong problem or premise that directed a focused answer

Use of prior knowledge, including principles as well as facts and events, for elaboration

Text references (i.e., Lincoln speech)

Explicit effort to show interrelationships

analyses reshaped our focus in a second major way. If we accepted that prior knowledge in subject matter was essential to both premise-driven and elaboration components of quality of understanding, then it was clear that we should design our assessment situations to include explicit supports to enable students to access such information. We believed that we could do this in any number of ways and decided to explore a range of options, details of which we will expose below. More importantly, we perceived that this decision dramatically revised our view of assessment. We decided that the assessment situation itself should help students to perform the best that they could. We had moved into the blurry territory between learning and testing.

Revising the situation. Our next step was to create new questions to relate to the class of expert behaviors we had proposed as criteria. We decided to have all students read both the Lincoln and the Douglas texts to permit them to use comparison as a rhetorical structure. We developed two variations of essay questions, or prompts, which we experimentally crossed: One treatment condition included a narrative context for the prompt and asked the student to imagine being in the pre-Civil War period and focus on an imaginary cousin as the audience for the essay; the other prompt presented the task as a more typical school assignment with the teachers as the implicit audience. A second set of treatments varied the instructions given to the student to assist their access to relevant prior knowledge. Although both conditions explicitly directed students to use their previous understanding and knowledge about the historical period in answering the essay question, one condition asked a series of stepped, short-answer questions to be completed before the student began to write the essay (see Table 8–5).

We also developed a prior-knowledge test, basing it on the broad model developed by Langer (1984), for two purposes. First, we wanted to help students access relevant prior knowledge; second, we wanted to look at the relationship between that measure and rated use of prior knowledge in the essay. This 20-item test was created using a set of specifications to control the nature of the content queried. Students were to write brief descriptions or definitions for each of the terms provided, some of which were facts and events (e.g., Dred Scott decision), and some of which were at the principle (or at least concept) level (e.g., sectionalism). A few terms were irrelevant to the passage, and some were only tangentially relevant.

The new test administration sequence required two days. On the first day the students were to complete a personal information form (including details about their interests, age, etc.) and the 20-item prior-knowledge measure. They then were to read the Lincoln and Douglas text segments and complete a short (14-item) multiple-choice test on information in the speeches. On the second day, they were to receive the essay question, write about 45 minutes, and complete a short debriefing questionnaire that asked for their reactions to the testing and for their estimates of their performance

TABLE 8-5. Sample Prompt: Step Narrative Version

Topic:

Imagine that it is 1858 and you are an educated citizen living in Illinois. Because you are interested in politics and always keep yourself well informed, you make a special trip to hear Abraham Lincoln and Stephen Douglas debating during their campaigns for the Senate seat representing Illinois.

1) Unlike other tests, we hope you really will try to imagine yourself in the historical period of the debates, so take a couple of minutes to describe yourself, your family, and your work. (Spend about 2–3 minutes.)

2) As a well-informed citizen, you are aware of the many important events, laws, and court decisions that relate to the debates. List as many of these as you can. (Spend about 3–4 minutes.)

3) List, if you can, some principles that underlie our form of government and that are relevant to the debate. (Spend 3–4 minutes.)

4) While listening to the debates, you begin to think about the major problems confronting the nation. Some of these problems relate to principles on which our government was founded. List the major problems you can think of. (Spend about 3–4 minutes.)

5) After the debates, you return home to find your cousin from England who has come to the U.S. for a visit. Your cousin asks you about some of the problems that are facing the nation at this time. Write the answer that you would give to your cousin, telling him/her about at least two problems that you feel are important. You can write this either like a regular essay or like a story. Just be sure to give your cousin the clearest picture you can. You may use any of the information you've identified above in your answer.

Be sure to descirbe each of the problems clearly and tell your cousin about events, laws, court decisions, and major principles of U.S. government that are related to the problem. Also explain the different solutions that are proposed to the problem, and give an example of what might happen if these solutions were adopted.

As a conclusion to your paper, write a brief summary that integrates the two problems and states your own position on the whole topic.

---

on the set of tasks tested. Following a pilot test in two Los Angeles classrooms, we tried the new assessment package in twelve classrooms in Springfield, Illinois.[1]

The Illinois Study

The purpose of the Illinois study was to test the assessment procedures under large-scale assessment conditions and to obtain data to bear on the validity of our findings. Here we have space for only a short description and discussion of this study. In brief, 250 students in eleventh grade participated, equally assigned from AP, college preparation, and regular classes. Two full class periods were allowed for the assessment. Students were told they were participating in a UCLA study to develop new measures for history. Since

[1] A good place for prior knowledge on Lincoln and Douglas.

there were four treatment variations (stepped essay prompts/short prompts/ narrative context/school context), students received their packets assigned at random within each classroom. On-site observers from UCLA administered the materials and collected information from teachers about their views of students' relative strengths in history, reading, test taking, and writing, and information about each teachers' instructional efforts in the topic area. In addition, we collected data from transcripts that reported students' course experience, grade-point averages, and standardized test scores in writing, social studies achievement and reading comprehension.

To obtain results, prior-knowledge scoring rubrics were developed and applied to student responses. Scores ranged from 3, a fully elaborated answer, to 1, an incorrect or incoherent response. Two graduate students were trained to use the prior-knowledge rubric and achieved 0.96 interrater reliability across the total measure (individual item agreements for the 20-item measure ranged between 0.70 and 0.96; 15 items had at least 0.86 agreement and only 2 fell below 0.80). Essays were rated using the new scoring rubric presented in Table 8–6.

This time our empirical results were encouraging. Interrater reliabilities for the essay subscales ranged between 0.85 and 0.98. Intercorrelations among subscales were found between 0.0 and 0.60, supporting the premise that different aspects of students' content quality were being assessed. Our findings also shed some light on the validity of the rubric. First, we determined that the measures reflected the different ability levels of the sample, with AP students scoring twice as high as the slower students on prior knowledge measures and on overall essay scores, and more than three times higher on use of principles in the essay. Our findings also showed strong relationships between teacher judgment of overall student achievement in history and our data ($r = 0.42$ for essay, 0.63 for prior knowledge). Our measures and standardized tests correlated 0.73 and 0.43, a variation based on standardized test content.

Scoring Criteria: Pass Four

We reviewed our findings and decided it was time to test whether regular history teachers could be trained to use the cognitive scoring scheme. We also decided to revise the scale in a number of ways: to add categories for

TABLE 8–6. Elements of Cognitively Sensitive Assessment Scoring Rubric

Problem focus
Prior knowledge: principles and facts
Text reference
General impression

TABLE 8-7. Cognitive Assessment Scoring Rubric (1989)

Presence of problem focus
Prior knowledge: principles
Prior knowledge: Facts and events
Text
Interrelationships
Misconceptions
General impression

---

misconceptions and interrelationships, since in our own discussions we had not found a place in our system to take such concerns into account; and to refine the scale points for principle and problem focus. The categories in the scoring rubric are displayed in Table 8-7.

We then conducted a training session with four high school history teachers to test the feasibility of our modified scoring approach. The training took approximately four hours, followed by the scoring session. Once again, we were very encouraged by our results. The prior knowledge measures and the essays were found to be reliably scored by teachers. Slightly lower interrater agreement overall was found for the high school teachers compared to the level obtained by project research assistants (alpha = 0.93 instead of 0.96). The interrater reliabilities on the essay subscales for teachers were in the 0.80–0.90 range, except for the newly added misconception category (0.68). Correlations between the prior-knowledge measure and related elements of the scoring scheme were all reasonably high, averaging around 0.59, except for misconceptions (-0.20) and text material (-0.28). We conducted a factor analysis on essay subscales, and two major factors emerged. One factor included overall scores on content quality, the use of principles-based prior-knowledge, premise-focused writing, and the interrelationships. The second factor included misconceptions, the use of facts, and the use of text-based material. Although we are not completely convinced that this factor structure is sensible, the configuration of elements as it relates to the cognitive construction of meaning (factor one) and of the application of disconnected, and perhaps incorrect information (factor two) is provocative.

NEXT STEPS

Research subsequent to the Illinois study has been undertaken to verify the utility of the scoring system across topics, age ranges, and test administration conditions. We are looking at the performance of ninth-, tenth-, and eleventh-grade students in two school districts. Data have been collected and are presently under analysis. The utility of this approach was tested using two additional assessment topics. Both of these topics are drawn from the pre-Revolutionary War period and include texts by Paine, Henry, and Inglis. In addition, new materials have been developed for an extended assignment that involves Long and Roosevelt texts from the Depression period and incorporates as well additional resource materials for students' optional use. We anticipate a total of five hours will be needed for the assessment.

Limitations and Cautions

We have recounted the details of this effort to provide some insight into how assessment systems might be developed to better reflect the ways students actually learn and integrate subject-matter material into their repertoires. We detailed our troubles and dead ends to demonstrate that the process of developing new kinds of useful and valid achievement measures is difficult and time consuming. New approaches to assessment are essential, but their development must be grounded in a theoretical view of learning. Establishing the validity of such new measures is also a difficult proposition. At least three major problems exist. One difficulty is the circular nature of new test development. Measures need to relate to but not be too strongly predicted by existing measurement strategies. A second problem with "deep-understanding" tasks is the clear lack of systematic experience for the average student. Most students reported to us that our tasks were unusual for them. Their overall performance levels were exceptionally poor. To determine if our measures are truly valid (that is, if they reflected the desired class of learning), experimental studies must be constructed in which students are trained explicitly in the process of integrating specifically presented material with various types of prior knowledge. Third, and most difficult, an optimal level of generality for task descriptions and scoring criteria is needed. This level must be sufficiently detailed to control raters' scoring behavior and to be valid for specific tasks. It must be sufficiently general to provide cues for teachers to use in planning and implementing instruction. A rough approximation of how such information can be economically displayed is provided in the specifications presented in Table 8-8. Such specifications would be augmented by detailed scoring rubrics with scale point definitions and also by a set of student papers illustrating, on different topics, various levels of proficiency. Clearly, a new program of psychometric research is needed. In the interim, we suggest that validity studies include criterion analyses by experts, experimental training studies, multiple measures of student learning processes, and demonstrations of statistical and conceptual connections to other reasonable estimates of performance, even including standardized tests.

TABLE 8-8. Specifications for Writing Tasks

Discourse Type
  Informative writing
Subgenre
  Explain/infer
Major Cognitive Process
  To demonstrate the acquisition of new knowledge or concept by contextualizing and elaborating position using prior knowledge (principles and facts)
Writing Process Measured
  Drafting
Audience
  Imaginary, peer
Topic Range
  Subject-matter based:
    History: A summary of major position by opposing statesmen
Information Given in Prompt
  History: Text of speeches or essays written by historical figures, e.g., Lincoln
Format
  Brief text
  Prior-knowledge cues: Consisting of appropriate and inappropriate terms for specific processes, facts, or principles
  Amount:
    2 or 3 pages (no more than 10 minutes of reading)
    A list of 10 or 20 entries for prior knowledge
Criteria
  Content:
    Organizing premise
    Explicit use of prior knowledge, principles, and facts (either provided or student generated) to explain or elaborate
    Avoidance of misconceptions
  Structure:
    Relevant text references
    Show interrelationships using text and prior information
Administrative Conditions
  Time: 45–60 minutes
  Resources: Students may refer to text and prior-knowledge list during essay preparation
  Interaction: None
Sample Prompt
  Segment of Patrick Henry's speech, plus list of prior-knowledge measure

Read the speech taken from the period just before the American Revolution. You are supposed to explain to a cousin visiting from Canada what Patrick Henry meant and what led him to the position he is in. Use help from the list of information to provide a clear answer.

Parallel Prompt

Same except pre-Civil War, Stephen Douglas

We know that tests have driven instruction in the past. Can tests of the sort we are developing do so in a productive rather than a destructive way? What evidence do we have that teachers of history focus on the integration of new knowledge with prior information—the view that learners construct meaning? Are such tasks within the capability of all students? When we are constantly bombarded with stories that students don't know where the Pacific Ocean is or in which half-century World War I occurred, is it naive to think that they can accumulate knowledge and use it to make inferences and explanations. These questions must be pursued. We believe that there are specific next steps to be accomplished. A major challenge is the development of a new theory of test design and validation, one that emphasizes individual learning rather than individual differences. Test designers must recognize that the measurement of significant processes takes significant time, and consequently tests of many short items and broad content sampling may need to be supplanted or supplemented by fewer, but more complex, assessment situations. We need to develop concepts that will allow teachers to understand how to use such measures as an integral part of their instruction. Finally, we must get ready for the serious task of educating policymakers and the public about new models of assessment. We must counsel patience and anticipate that results are going to look worse, especially with new challenging measurement approaches, before they look better. When improvements eventually occur on cognitive measures such as those we have explored, we want them to reflect real and trustworthy learning for all students.

REFERENCES

ANDERSON, R.C., SPIRO, R.J., & ANDERSON, M.C. (1978). Schemata as scaffolding for the representation of information in connected discourse. *American Educational Research Journal, 15,* 433–440.
BAKER, E.L. (1987, September). *Time to write.* Paper presented at the Annual Meeting of the International Education Association, New York.
BAKER, E.L., & QUELLMALZ, E.S. (1980, April). *Issues in eliciting writing performance: Problems in alternative prompting strategies.* Paper presented at the annual meeting of the National Council on Measurement in Education, Boston.
BECK, I.L., McKEOWN, M.G., & GROMOLL, E.W. (1989). Learning from social studies texts. *Cognitions and Instruction, 6*(2), 99–158.
BROWN, A.L., BRANSFORD, J.D., FERRARA, R.A., & CAMPIONE, J.C. (1983). Learning, remembering, and understanding. In P.H. Mussen (Ed.), *Handbook of child psychology, Vol. 3.: Cognitive development* (pp. 77–166). New York: Wiley.

152   *Cognitive Assessment of History for Large-Scale Testing*

CANNELL, J.J. (1987). *Nationally normed elementary achievement testing in America's public schools: How all 50 states are above the national average* (2nd ed.). Daniels, WV: Friends for Education.

CHI, M.T.H., & GLASER, R. (1980). The measurement of expertise: Analysis of the development of knowledge and skill as a basis for assessing achievement. In E.L. Baker & E.S. Quellmalz (Eds.), *Educational testing and evaluation: Design, analysis, and policy.* Beverly Hills, CA: Sage.

FITZGERALD, F. (1979). *America revised: What history textbooks have taught our children about their country, and how and why those textbooks have changed in different decades.* New York: Vintage.

FLODEN, R.E., PORTER, A.C., SCHMIDT, W.H., & FREEMAN, D.J. (1980). Don't they all measure the same thing? Consequences of standardized test selection. In E.L. Baker & E.S. Quellmalz (Eds.), *Educational testing and evaluation: Design, analysis, and policy.* Beverly Hills, CA: Sage.

HIRSCH, E.D., KETT, J., & TREFIL, J. (1987). *Cultural literacy: What every American needs to know.* Boston: Houghton Mifflin.

KIERAS, D.E. (1985). Thematic processes in the comprehension of technical prose. In B.K. Britton & J.B. Black (Eds.), *Understanding expository text: A theoretical and practical handbook for analyzing explanatory text* (pp. 89–107). Hillsdale, NJ: Lawrence Erlbaum.

LANGER, J.A. (1984). Pre-reading plan (PRep): Facilitating text comprehension. In J. Chapman (Ed.), *The reader and the text.* London: Heinemann.

LINN, R.L., GRAUE, M.E., & SANDERS, N. (1989). *Comparing state and district test results to national norms: Interpretations of scoring "above the national average"* (CSE Technical Report 308). Los Angeles: UCLA Center for the Study of Evaluation.

National Assessment of Educational Progress. (1990). *The nation's writing report card.* Princeton, NJ: Educational Testing Service.

National Commission for Educational Excellence. (1983). *A nation at risk.* Washington, DC: U.S. Government Printing Office.

OAKES, J. (1986, October). Keeping track, part 2: Curriculum inequality and school reform. *Phi Delta Kappan,* 68(2), 148–154.

POPHAM, J. (1990, January). *Appropriateness of teachers' test-preparation practices.* Paper presented at a Forum for Dialogues Between Educational Policy Makers and Educational Researchers, University of California, Los Angeles.

POPHAM, W.J., & HUSEK, T.R. (1969). Implications of criterion-referenced measurement. *Journal of Educational Measurement, 6,* 1–9.

QUELLMALZ, E.S., CAPELL, F., & CHOU, C. (1982). Defining writing domains: Effects of discourse and response mode. *Journal of Educational Measurement, 19,* 241–258.

QUELLMALZ, E.S. (1986). Writing skills assessment. In R.A. Berk (Ed.), *Performance assessment: Methods and applications.* Baltimore: Johns Hopkins University Press.

QUELLMALZ, E.S., SMITH, L.S., WINTERS, L.S., & BAKER, E.L. (1980). *Characteristics of student writing competence: An investigation of alternative scoring systems* (Report to the National Institute of Education). Los Angeles: UCLA Center for the Study of Evaluation.

RAVITCH, D., & FINN, C.E. (1987). *What do our 17-year-olds know?: A report on the first national assessment of history and literature.* New York: Harper & Row.

RUMELHART, D.E. (1980). Schemata: The building of blocks of cognition. In R.J. Spiro, B.C. Bruce, & W.F. Brewer (Eds.), *Theoretical issues in reading comprehension* (pp. 33–58). Hillsdale, NJ: Lawrence Erlbaum.

SEWALL, G.T. (1987). *American history textbooks: An assessment of quality.* New York: Educational Excellence Network.

SHEPARD, L. (1989). *Is it old norms, or teaching the test?* (CSE Technical Report 307). Los Angeles: UCLA Center for the Study of Evaluation.

SMITH, L.S. (1978, November). *Investigation of writing assessment strategies* (Report to the National Institute of Education). Los Angeles: UCLA Center for the Study of Evaluation.

STRENIO, A.J. (1981). *The testing trap: How it can make or break your career and your children's futures.* New York: Rawson, Wade.

VAUGHAN, A.T. (1983). *Grading the advanced placement examinations in American history.* Princeton, NJ: College Entrance Examination Board.

VOSS, J. (1978). Strategic difficulties in summarizing texts. *Reading Research Quarterly, 19,* 404–426.

WITTROCK, M.C. (1974). Learning as a generative process. *Educational Psychologist, 11,* 87–95.

WITTROCK, M.C. (1990). Generative processes of comprehension. *Educational Psychologist, 24,* 345–376.

NINE

RESEARCH IN COGNITION AND LEARNING: IMPLICATIONS FOR ACHIEVEMENT TESTING PRACTICE

Joan L. Herman

Joan L. Herman reflects on the ideas and suggestions developed by the authors of the chapters of this book. To these ideas and suggestions she adds some of her own insights and discusses some future directions for achievement testing. Assessment practices in schools will change substantially and productively by focusing upon improving instruction through assessing student cognitive processes, student preconceptions, and the learning of relationships and structures. These measures will help to identify the causes of problems in learning, and will facilitate the design of instructionally effective teaching strategies.

Robert Glaser sagely articulates an underlying assumption for the explorations of this volume. "The [value of] assessment systems we derive depend intimately on our knowledge of how humans learn and acquire knowledge and skill . . ." (p. 18). How valuable are our current assessment systems judged from this perspective? Glaser and the other authors in this volume explicate advances in cognitive theory and new understandings of the learning process that should give us pause for concern. Their perspectives raise fundamental questions about the meaning of scores derived from existing standardized tests and about the validity of the assumptions underlying their development and interpretation. The collection points the way to more valuable testing systems grounded more firmly in our understandings of how students learn. The authors' recommendations also evoke considerations of the content and nature of effective assessment approaches that can assist in the improvement of student learning.

THE MEANING OF RESULTS FROM STANDARDIZED TESTS

Aptitude Versus Skill Development

A first question about the meaning of test results is a very basic one about presumed distinctions in major categories of tests. While most elementary texts on measurement cite three basic varieties of tests—aptitude, achievement, and attitude—it seems clear from the chapters in this volume that the distinction is getting murky. An aptitude test such as a standard IQ measure is supposed to measure potential, and in common practice that potential is assumed to be relatively immutable, stable across time and generalizable across a full gamut of content areas, disciplines, and areas of endeavor. These qualities largely justify the use of aptitude tests for selection purposes. An achievement test, in contrast, is supposed to measure learning attainment, presumably both malleable over time (within the limits of aptitude) and domain or content specific. The research described in this book disperses such simple-minded definitions and more—raises exciting possibilities and assumptions about human potential.

The good news is that what we used to think of as aptitude may well be more malleable than once thought. Research on metacognition and learning strategies suggests that we can teach students to learn, and that what the uninitiated once thought of as basic ability is actually trainable. What Weinstein defines as teachable learning strategies bears strong resemblance to some components of Sternberg's Componential subtheory. And in fact, Weinstein and her colleagues (1988) as well as Brown, Bransford, Ferrara, and Campione, among others, have had notable success in training students in learning strategies.

At the higher end of the spectrum, the border line between intelligence and achievement in domain-independent problem solving (if there is such a thing) similarly is moot. Distinctions aside, similar levels of optimism seem to pervade both many intelligence theorists and many learning and instruction researchers: Underlying the conceptions of both camps is an assumption that if we can understand human performance, we then can test and diagnose it and subsequently find ways to design interventions and strategies to improve it.

The Many Factors That Influence Performance

The bad news is, given the complexity of the processes underlying performance, what meaning can we really derive from a student's performance on a current standardized achievement test? The chapters of this book remind us that performance on any particular task is a function, not only of ability and skill, but of a variety of other factors as well: attention (Wittrock), motivation (Wittrock, Weinstein, Meyer, McCombs), anxiety, and external contingencies, among other things. Measurement experts, researchers, and anyone who has observed in classrooms on standardized test days—for example, watched an adolescent create innovative patterns on his or her answer sheet—know this shortcoming well. However, many constituencies who are intended to use achievement testing for decision making may well be lacking this basic understanding.

Legislators, other decision makers, the public, parents, even to some extent teachers and administrators, seem to believe that test results tell them something straightforward about students' achievement. While many of these people are sophisticated enough to know that tests cannot cover all that is important in schooling or even all that is important in cognitive learning (Herman, Winters, & Golan, 1989), they appear to trust that a particular score reflects what students are able to achieve—and not simply what they are willing to demonstrate. For some segments of the population, the willing, or motivated-to-demonstrate dimension may well seriously skew results and similarly impair any decisions that are made based on those results.

The Substantive Meaning of Test Results

Those who are not measurement experts also frequently misconceive the meaning of the common standardized, norm-referenced tests. They assume that scores presented relative to some national average—whether they be grade equivalent, percentile, stanine, or standard—have substantive, criterion-referenced meaning relative to what students can and cannot do. Scoring at the fifth-grade level, they believe, means that students have achieved a particular body of knowledge. The conceptions of learning, development, and skill raised in this book underscore the seriousness of such misconceptions.

Misinterpretations of the meaning of norm-referenced findings aside, the perspectives articulated in this book raise serious questions about the construct validity of our tests and their generalizability. If student performance is domain specific, then getting a smattering of information about performance in a number of domain areas, as many standardized tests currently do, is insufficient to reliably determine the nature of student performance in any single domain or across domains. What do current tests really tell us? Generally they simply tell us that students who know a lot in a general area know a lot relative to their peers, and that students who do not know a lot do not know much relative to their peers. But what do they know (or not know)? To get an answer to the latter question, we need to get more domain-specific information—and to do that, we will need more systematically to sample performance within specified domains, meaning significantly more time in assessment to get stable estimates.

How specific is domain specific? This is a serious and perplexing problem for determining the level at which we should be defining domains for test development. Should we be specifying at the level of science? Within science as physics, biology, or the like? Within physics at the level of thermodynamics, Boyle's Law, Ohm's Law, and so forth? The answers to such specification questions will vary with the level at which results are intended to be reported and used. For example, while policymakers and the public may feel satisfied simply knowing how students are doing in science, if teachers are going to take targeted instructional action, they will need detailed information on performance (not relative standing) in specific areas.

Problems in Generalizability of Performance

Problematic issues in generalizability pervade the test-specification process and the interpretability of any results. For example, is there such a thing as "scientific reasoning"? Will/does it generalize across science disciplines? Across topics within discipline? Across difference performance tasks? While learning theorists struggle with such questions, tests appear to be developed and their results interpreted as though these questions do not exist. Nonetheless, the validity of our assessments as measures of human performance is constrained by our understanding of both human performance and the structure of content domains.

Research in performance testing demonstrates how fragile is the generalizability of performance. For example, consider performance in writing. Research conducted at the Center for Research on Evaluation, Standards, and Student Testing (CRESST) indicates that writing skill does not generalize across genres, so that a good writer is not a good writer regardless of the nature of the writing task (Quellmalz, Capell, & Chou, 1982). Further, this same research shows that within genre, clear topic effects are observed, so that even good descriptive writers are not good writers regardless of the specific writing task. Where does this leave us in drawing strong conclusions from the results of an assessment? The results in the National Assessment of

Educational Progress' *Writing Trends Across the Decade, 1974-84* (Applebee, Langer, & Mullis, 1986) are instructive. The report documents trends in student writing over three data points in three different genres: informative, persuasive, and imaginative writing. Because of changes in both writing prompts and in administrative procedures over the three assessment periods, student responses from only one prompt per genre were available for the three-year trend analysis. Thus, the meaning that can be derived from these findings is directly proportional to our confidence that each prompt adequately represents students' performance in each genre.

To what extent is each prompt representative in this sense? Not sufficiently, based on evidence presented in the NAEP report itself. Significantly different pictures of student skill levels emerge depending on which of several prompts available in a single year is used. Looking at the 1974 and 1979 assessment of nine-year-olds, for example, we find that the percentage of students rated minimal or better in persuasive writing in one year ranges from about 35% to 75%, depending on the prompt chosen to characterize their performance (Applebee, Langer, & Mullis, 1986, p. 45). The trend data also lead to different conclusions depending on the prompts selected for scrutiny. Looking at the performance of thirteen-year-olds on imaginative tasks, we find that two of the three prompts show a slight upward trend from 1974 to 1979; but the third one, and the one upon which the three-year trend analysis is based, evidences a downward trend over the same period.

Continuing Problems in Content Validity

While some people might argue that averaging students' performance over a number of items, as is the case in multiple-choice tests, alleviates some of these generalizability problems, problems in content validity still remain. Under typical standardized test development processes, the nature of the domain to which performance is supposed to generalize is left largely unspecified. Rather than starting a priori with a detailed, well-grounded conception of a knowledge or skill domain, one is arrived at post hoc, based on empirical data. Consider the typical process (see House, 1989): content experts, curriculum specialists, teachers, and others are gathered together to reach consensus on the general topics and processes that are to be assessed. The result is a general content-process matrix that becomes the basis for generating large numbers of test items. The items so generated are then subjected to both empirical and judgmental procedures; the surviving items, those which are both empirically coherent and judged representative of something important, are then assumed to adequately define the domain of interest. The item writers and the test items themselves, in short, define de facto the domain being measured.

The surviving items usually cover a variety of specific topics, with any single item typically measuring only a minuscule fraction of a specific topic (and with the specifics it measures left to the discretion of the item writer, hidden from public view). While content validation procedures help to assure that items included on the test are considered important, what assurance is there that the test items represent the full range of important, relevant content? Have items been sampled broadly to fully represent the domain of interest, or are test items concentrated in particular areas and in a constricted, but unknown, skill range? Figure 9–1 displays alternative pictures of how well a given number of test items may cover a domain.

What Actually Is Measured?

While one hopes for the most comprehensive and balanced picture of domain coverage,the reality may be distorted. Tests of empirical coherence typically employed in the development of multiple-choice assessments, in fact, may mitigate against a fully balanced representation and instead support a more constricted view of a given skill or knowledge domain. The difficulty of using multiple-choice items to measure deep understanding and the highest levels of cognitive skill is frequently acknowledged. Demonstrating the limits of using multiple-choice items to measure higher-level production skill, early studies at UCLA's Center for the Study of Evaluation (Spooner-Smith, 1980, for example) found that students' performance on multiple-choice tests of writing skill did not adequately predict their actual performance in writing, even when both measures were directed at the same analytic skill categories.

Taken together, these two observations (i.e., the difficulty of developing test items to measure the highest levels of cognitive skill and the inadequacies of recognition items for measuring complex production tasks) point to an important flaw in relying heavily upon empirical coherence to validate a set of items. Within any given field test of multiple-choice items, only a few might be expected to be written creatively enough to assess high-level production skills and/or problem-solving; conversely, because they are easier to conceive and construct, items assessing lower-level skills might be expected to occur with great frequency. Those items that are empirically coherent, then, may well be concentrated in lower levels of skill application and miss the most complex aspects of problem solving. Furthermore, some of those

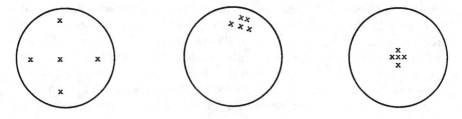

FIGURE 9-1. Representations of Domain Coverage

items that are discarded as outliers may, in fact, capture something of real significance.

Are We Measuring What Is Most Important?

Glaser's comments on expert-novice distinctions are both germane and disturbing here. According to Glaser, one important distinction between experts and novices is not their competence in recalling small, specific items of domain-related information, but rather their ability to discern and apply meaningful patterns of behavior in pursuit of complex goals. One might wonder how likely current tests are to capture such critical components of expertise.

Even if one assumes that the public school's mission is not to produce "experts" but rather to educate "skilled novices," the accumulated knowledge of cognitive psychology (see also the chapters by Sternberg, Weinstein, and Wittrock) suggests that the presence or absence of discrete bits of information is not what is of primary importance in meaningful learning, but rather how and whether that information is organized, structured, and used in context. Further, contrary to the typical piecemeal and decontextualized items found on most multiple-choice tests, developments in almost every field suggest the importance of the dynamic unity, not the mechanical collection of things (Lucas, 1985).

TOWARD BETTER TESTS OF ACHIEVEMENT

While they raise questions about the meaning of current tests and their development procedures, the arguments above also sow the seeds of a solution: test-design procedures fully grounded in what is known about meaningful learning and skilled performance.

Specifications Based in Learning Research

Key to improving the meaningfulness and interpretability of test results are test development procedures which specify a priori the operational characteristics of the domain(s) to be assessed. This call for greater descriptive rigor is not new, but echoes early and continuing advocacies for criterion-referenced, domain-referenced, mastery, and competency-based tests (Glaser, 1963, Popham & Husek, 1969; Hively, 1973; Millman, 1974). Combining specification procedures with research in learning, instruction, and cognitive science, Baker and Herman (1983) proposed a design approach based on the definition of task structures; these research-based structures then provide specific, descriptive, and generalizable blueprints against which test items can be generated.

While Baker and Collis and Romberg in this book provide examples of new assessments so designed for social studies and mathematics respectively,

Glaser, Sternberg, and Wittrock explicate concepts that could be used to specify achievement tests across content areas. For example, three of the indicators of competence articulated by Glaser—the coherence of knowledge, the extent of principled problem solving, and the usability of knowledge—offer a way to classify the types of assessment tasks that need to be designed to assess students' skill in any specific area. Moving beyond these general concepts to generalizable, operational definitions and validated assessments, however, will require sustained attention to substantive design and psychometric issues. Baker's content-assessment work exemplifies the intellectual effort that needs to be brought to bear, and in fact her assessment scheme addresses dimensions very similar to those raised by Glaser. Further, consistent with points made by Glaser, Sternberg, and Weinstein, the scheme also differentiates the assessment of knowledge-based and reasoning-based performance in the context of complex, integrative tasks. If scales such as hers generalize across topics and subject areas, they will offer both potent tools and viable models for mapping the instruction and the assessment across the curriculum.

The Value of Complex Assessment Tasks

Baker makes a strong case for assessments based in integrative performance tasks. Beyond their value in assuring that assessments reflect meaningful, higher-level thinking skills and do not trivialize the learning process, such tasks also provide a multipurpose context for deriving a variety of assessments. For example, while Baker's current scale includes, among other things, measures of levels and structure of knowledge, one might also imagine subscales dealing with students' reasoning process, analytic and synthetic thinking, and so forth. For large-scale assessment purposes, the reliability of individual estimates on such scales is likely to be highly problematic in the absence of repeated, time-consuming, and relatively costly individual samples. Such familiar arguments have supported the continued use of multiple-choice tests for standardized and large-scale assessment. The argument being advanced here, however, is that issues of what it is that is being assessed and the level, significance, and meaningfulness of what is assessed are at least equally as important as the issue of getting reliable individual student scores.

Differentiating Various Assessment Purposes

Furthermore, for policy, monitoring, and accountability purposes, reliable individual scores may be an unnecessary luxury. As a variety of state assessments in writing and NAEP demonstrates, group estimates on a variety of tasks are both feasible and effective for these purposes. Although individual diagnostic information is lost, time- and cost-efficient assessments potentially useful in curricular review and program improvement as well as accountability are gained.

The push-pull between desires for more authentic kinds of assessment and the time and expense they require means we need to moderate ideals of multipurpose, instructionally relevant tests that can serve simultaneously individual, classroom, school, district, and state decision-making needs. Overlapping strategies, potentially built on common assessment models, may offer both a better match to current reality and a more productive model for future assessment policy and practice. Under such a model, results from large-scale assessment serving district, state, and/or national needs are expected to serve a function they are capable of serving: providing only a signal regarding how well students are doing in a particular area. Should the signal indicate the need for improvement and/or the area assessed be a particular priority, then the local school is responsible for following up with more detailed, perhaps individually based, assessments that are the basis for program prescriptions and/or individual remediation and action. Responsibility for locating the source or reasons for performance difficulties, be they in program or individual problems, then rests in the hands of local professionals, using professional tools at their disposal (including formal assessments, informal inventories and observations, professional analysis and judgment) customized to their local curriculum and priorities.

Research shows that operating reality is already close to this picture in that teachers and principals rely very little on formal standardized tests or large-scale assessments in their planning and decision making and use instead their own tests and observations (Dorr-Bremme & Herman, 1986; Smith Edelsley, Draper, Rottenberg, & Cherland, 1989). However, research also shows that another part of the picture has yet to be adequately developed: the systematic use of formal and informal data in program planning and improvement. Sirotnik, Dorr-Bremme, and Burstein, (1986) differentiate between social and clinical uses of information in schools, where *clinical* refers to the diagnostic use of formal information for individual prescription, and *social* refers to uses of group data for planning and decision making at class and school levels. Sirotnik and others have noted that, while educators are both familiar and at least rhetorically committed to clinical uses, social uses generally are not part of their operating schema (Sirotnik, Dorr-Bremme, & Burstein, 1986; Herman, Winters, & Golan, 1989). Further, perhaps partially because of this bias, local educators tend not to value, nor to find credible, assessments that do not yield individual student scores. The model being proposed, therefore, has implications for training teachers and administrators in the use of data for program planning and school improvement.

MATCHING ASSESSMENT STRATEGIES
WITH CURRENT REALITIES

On the one hand, for quality monitoring we need assessments that can help indicate general areas of strength and weakness. On the other hand, we need more intensive assessments, which help educators identify the specific causes of problems, their underlying causes, and change strategies for their improvement at the individual, class, program, and school levels. The authors in this book have described some of the important dimensions constructing and influencing human cognition and performance that are relevant to this second level of assessment. They have argued for better, presumably formal and standardized, measures of these constructs for use in classroom instruction and instructional decision making. That a construct influences learning and performance, however, does not mean that routine formal testing is required—the aims of research and of understanding learning require such measures, but do routine instructional planning and decision making require them as well? Planning and instructional delivery can take such variables into account in the absence of formal, diagnostic data.

If teachers are the intended users, it would be well to consider what is known about how educators use or do not use formal assessment data before recommending the development of new instruments. From this perspective, and because of problems in performance transfer from one topical setting to the next, the utility and validity of traditional standard measures are moot. Further, given the plethora of variables that are thought to be important determinants of learning and performance, the cost-benefit tradeoff of separate formal assessment also warrants consideration.

It might be better to consider how best to encourage teachers to incorporate selected cognitive and noncognitive variables into their routine planning, instructional delivery, and informal assessment strategies. For example, rather than formally assessing (and attempting to disentangle) students' learning strategies, affect, attention, and so on, a more utilitarian course may be to assure that teachers take into account these variables as they design their instruction and be attentive and reflect on how well their instructional sequences meet their cognitive and other objectives. For instance, if many students are having difficulty, strategies to increase attention and motivation and also teach or incorporate explicit learning strategies may be employed simultaneously. Such an approach may be experimentally inelegant, but practically both more realistic and more effective in improving instructional effectiveness.

Assessment is a natural ally in clinical or other systematic planning approaches to instructional delivery. This natural base, however, often is missing in actual teaching practice. Requisite to more serious use of assessment data for instructional improvement and/or to the incorporation of important cognitive and noncognitive variables into such assessments, thus, are sustained professional development and training efforts to foster clinical teaching and/or other systematic planning approaches. Once such a base is established, what kinds of tests or assessments might best serve teachers' needs? As noted above, research repeatedly shows teachers' minimal use of measures that originate outside their classrooms, their activity-oriented planning, and their penchant for assessment that is grounded in classroom instruction (Dorr-Bremme, 1983; Dorr-Bremme and Herman, 1986). Building additionally from what we know about the information sources teachers most rely on—their own observations and professional judgment—and on the opportunities routine classroom instruction provides for repeated observations of student performance (through discussion, classroom assignments, worksheets, etc.), generalized assessment "templates" might represent a more valid and useful assessment strategy than do typical static measures. As Baker's content assessment scheme demonstrates, rather than being a single measure, these templates can articulate the important dimensions of higher-level skill proficiency applicable across specific topics in one curriculum area (or potentially even across curricula) and thus be applicable repeatedly across and within specific classroom content. Furnishing a conceptual schema for analyzing skill development, templates could be incorporated formally and informally into classroom assignments as well as tests.

The strength of a template type of approach is demonstrated in some states' and districts' experience in writing assessment. In one example, the district adopted an analytic scoring scale for minimum competency purposes and widely trained teachers in the use of the scale. Beyond a formal tool for evaluating student competency at critical points, the scale also began to be widely used by teachers in their classrooms, focusing instruction on critical features and providing teachers with an easy, efficient way to grade and provide feedback to their students. Assessment was integrated into routine instructional practice with one observed result being an improvement in students' writing over time (Quellmalz & Burry, 1983).

In conclusion, the chapters of this book raise vexing problems about the meaning of current standardized tests as well as interesting possibilities for the future of assessment. Based on research in human learning and cognition, one thing is certain about current achievement testing practice: As Sternberg admonishes us, "We can do better." (p. 32)

REFERENCES

APPLEBEE, A.N., LANGER, J.A., & MULLIS, I.V.S. (1986). *Writing trends across the decade, 1974–84* (National Assessment of Educational Progress Report No. 15-W-01). Princeton, NJ: Educational Testing Service.

BROWN, A.L., BRANSFORD, J.F., FERRARA, R., & CAMPIONE, J. (1983). Learning, remembering, and understanding. In J. Flavell & E. Markman (Eds.), *Handbook of child psychology* (Vol. 3, pp. 77–166). New York: Wiley.

BAKER, E.L. (1990). [this volume]

BAKER, E.L., & HERMAN, J.L. (1983). Task structure design: Beyond linkage. *Journal of Educational Management, 20*(2), 149–164.

COLLIS, K., & ROMBERG, T. [this volume]

DORR-BREMME, D.W. (1983). Assessing students: Teachers' routine practices and reasoning. *Evaluation Comment, 6*(4), 1–12.

DORR-BREMME, D.W., & HERMAN, J.L. (1986). *Assessing student achievement: A profile of classroom practices* (CSE Monograph Series in Evaluation No. 11). Los Angeles: UCLA Center for the Study of Evaluation.

GLASER, R. (1963). Instructional technology and the measurement of learning: Some questions. *American Psychologist*, 18, 519–521.

GLASER, R. (1990). [this volume]

HERMAN, J.L., WINTERS, L., & GOLAN, S. (1989). *Reporting for effective decisionmaking* (CSE Tech. Rep. No. 298). Los Angeles: UCLA Center for the Study of Evaluation.

HERMAN, J.L. (Ed.). (1983). *Educational testing and evaluation: Critical research and development needs* (CSE Tech. Rep. No. 213). Los Angeles: UCLA Center for the Study of Evaluation.

HIVELY, W. (1973). *Domain-referenced curriculum evaluation: A technical handbook and a case study from the Minnemast project* (CSE Monograph Series in Evaluation No. 1). Los Angeles: UCLA Center for the Study of Evaluation.

HOUSE, E.R. (1989). *Report on content definition process in social studies testing* (CSE Tech. Rep. No. 309). Los Angeles: UCLA Center for the Study of Evaluation.

LUCAS, C. (1985). Out at the edge: Notes on a paradigm shift. *Journal of Counseling and Development*, 64, 165–172.

MCCOMBS, B.L. (1990). [this volume]

MILLMAN, J. (1974). Criterion-referenced measurement. In W. J. Popham (Ed.), *Evaluation in education: Current applications* (pp. 311–377). Berkeley, CA: McCutchan.

POPHAM, W.J., & HUSEK, T. (1969). Implications of criterion-referenced measurement. *Journal of Educational Measurement*, 6, 1–9.

QUELLMALZ, E.S., CAPELL, F.J., & CHOU, C.P. (1982). Defining writing: Effects of discourse and response mode. *Journal of Educational Measurement*, 14, 4.

QUELLMALZ, E.S., & BURRY, J. (1983). *Analytic scales for assessing students' expository and narrative writing skills* (CSE Resource Paper No. 5). Los Angeles: UCLA Center for the Study of Evaluation.

SIROTNIK, K., DORR-BREMME, D.W., & BURSTEIN, L. (1986). *Social vs. clinical perspectives on the use of information: Implications for school-based information systems* (CSE Tech. Rep. No. 258). Los Angeles: UCLA Center for the Study of Evaluation.

SMITH, M.L., EDELSKY, C., DRAPER, K., ROTTENBERG, C., & CHERLAND, M. (1989). *The natural history of the testing event* (Report to OERI, Grant No. G-86-0003). Los Angeles: UCLA Center for the Study of Evaluation.

SPOONER-SMITH, L. (1980). *Investigation of writing assessment strategies* (CSE Tech. Rep. No. 133). Los Angeles: UCLA Center for the Study of Evaluation.

STERNBERG, R. (1990). [this volume]

WEINSTEIN, C.E., & MAYER, R.E. (1985). The teaching of learning strategies. In. M.C. Wittrock (Ed.), *Handbook of research on teaching* (3rd ed.). New York: Macmillan.

WEINSTEIN, C.E., GOETZ, E.T., & ALEXANDER, P.A. (Eds.). (1988). *Learning and study strategies: Issues in assessment, instruction, and evaluation*. New York: Academic Press.

WEINSTEIN, C.E. (1990). [this volume]

WITTROCK, M.C. (1986). Students' thought processes. In M.C. Wittrock (Ed.), *Handbook of research on teaching* (3rd ed.). New York: Macmillan.

WITTROCK, M.C. (1990). [this volume]

INDEX

Postformal mode of functioning, mathematics in, 98
Practical intelligence, 36–37
Pressley, M., 41, 43, 55, 57
Primary motivational processes, 62–81
future research on, 72–75
potential self-system measures, 76–78
research on, 64–71
self-system variables, 71–72
Principled problem solving, and competence, 27
Prior knowledge:
importance of, 42, 46
successful vs. unsuccessful learners, 54–55
Problem representation:
and expert performance, 20–21
and writing expertise, 25–26
Problem solving, and mathematics, 84
Procedural knowledge:
successful vs. unsuccessful learners, 54–55
and writing expertise, 24–25

Q

Qualitative analysis, and reasoning abilities, 21–22
Quellmalz, E. S., 136, 139, 140, 141, 157, 164

R

Raizen, S. A., 85
Ravitch, D., 136
Reading:
comprehension, 8–9
inconsistencies, detection of, 46
Reasoning, and mathematics, 84
Recht, D. R., 42
Rees, E., 20, 34, 42, 54, 86
Reid, D., 77
Reif, F., 56
Relational characteristic, concrete-symbolic mode, 116
Relich, J., 67, 76, 77
Representation, and writing expertise, 25–26

Resnick, L. B., 94, 95
Richards, F. A., 98
Rieser, J., 12
Rogers, T. B., 46, 64, 68
Romberg, T. A., 83, 95
Rottenberg, C., 162
Rotter, J. B., 77
Rumelhart, D. E., 138
Russell, 78
Ryan, R. M., 64, 65, 66

S

Saari, L. M., 57
Salomon, G., 42, 55, 56
Sanders, N., 134
Scheier, R. R., 68
Schemas, 45, 72
Schliemann, A. D., 94
Schmeck, R. R., 41, 42, 68
Schmidt, W. H., 133
School Concerns Scale, 77
Schriver, K., 25
Schulte, A. C., 49
Schultze, H. J., 14
Schunk, D. H., 41, 56, 57, 65, 66, 68, 73
Schwartz, B. J., 20
Scoring, test items, 114–15
Scribner, S., 94
Sears, P. S., 76
Segal, J., 86
Self-Description Questionnaire, 76
Self-Efficacy Measure, 76
Self-evaluations, 65
Self-monitoring skills, experts vs. novices, 46
Self-Perceptions Profile for Adolescents, 76
Self-regulatory skills, and competence, 27–28
Self-system/self-regulated learning, 71–78
and affect, 69–71
and motivation, 68–69, 71–72
self-referent nature of filtering process of, 66–68
structure of, 64–66
Sensorimotor mode of functioning, 87–89, 91, 116
Sentis, K., 65
Sewall, G. T., 138
Shavelson, R. J., 9, 64